T0210639

Probabilistic Ranking Techniques in Relational Databases

Probabilistic Ranking Techniques in Relational Databases
Ihab F. Ilyas and Mohamed A. Soliman

ISBN: 978-3-031-00718-7   paperback
ISBN: 978-3-031-01846-6   ebook

DOI 10.1007/978-3-031-01846-6

A Publication in the Springer series
SYNTHESIS LECTURES ON DATA MANAGEMENT

Lecture #14
Series Editor: M. Tame Özsu, *University of Waterloo*
Series ISSN
Synthesis Lectures on Data Management
Print 2153-5418   Electronic 2153-5426

Synthesis Lectures on Data Management

Editor

M. Tame Özsu, *University of Waterloo*

Synthesis Lectures on Data Management is edited by Tamer Özsu of the University of Waterloo. The series will publish 50- to 125 page publications on topics pertaining to data management. The scope will largely follow the purview of premier information and computer science conferences, such as ACM SIGMOD, VLDB, ICDE, PODS, ICDT, and ACM KDD. Potential topics include, but not are limited to: query languages, database system architectures, transaction management, data warehousing, XML and databases, data stream systems, wide scale data distribution, multimedia data management, data mining, and related subjects.

Probabilistic Ranking Techniques in Relational Databases
Ihab F. Ilyas and Mohamed A. Soliman
2011

Uncertain Schema Matching
Avigdor Gal
2011

Fundamentals of Object Databases: Object-Oriented and Object-Relational Design
Suzanne W. Dietrich and Susan D. Urban
2010

Advanced Metasearch Engine Technology
Weiyi Meng and Clement T. Yu
2010

Web Page Recommendation Models: Theory and Algorithms
Sule Gündüz-Ögüdücü
2010

Multidimensional Databases and Data Warehousing
Christian S. Jensen, Torben Bach Pedersen, and Christian Thomsen
2010

Probabilistic Ranking Techniques in Relational Databases

Ihab F. Ilyas
University of Waterloo

Mohamed A. Soliman
Greenplum

SYNTHESIS LECTURES ON DATA MANAGEMENT #14

ABSTRACT

Ranking queries are widely used in data exploration, data analysis and decision making scenarios. While most of the currently proposed ranking techniques focus on deterministic data, several emerging applications involve data that are imprecise or uncertain. Ranking uncertain data raises new challenges in query semantics and processing, making conventional methods inapplicable. Furthermore, the interplay between ranking and uncertainty models introduces new dimensions for ordering query results that do not exist in the traditional settings.

This lecture describes new formulations and processing techniques for ranking queries on uncertain data. The formulations are based on marriage of traditional ranking semantics with possible worlds semantics under widely-adopted uncertainty models. In particular, we focus on discussing the impact of tuple-level and attribute-level uncertainty on the semantics and processing techniques of ranking queries.

Under the tuple-level uncertainty model, we describe new processing techniques leveraging the capabilities of relational database systems to recognize and handle data uncertainty in score-based ranking. Under the attribute-level uncertainty model, we describe new probabilistic ranking models and a set of query evaluation algorithms, including sampling-based techniques. We also discuss supporting rank join queries on uncertain data, and we show how to extend current rank join methods to handle uncertainty in scoring attributes.

KEYWORDS

ranking, uncertainty, probabilistic models, query processing, top-k, partial order, probabilistic database, uncertain databases, ranking semantics

Contents

CHAPTER 1

Introduction

Ranking queries are widely used in data exploration, data analysis and decision making scenarios. The objective of ranking queries (also referred to as top-k queries) is to report the top ranked query results, based on scores computed by a given scoring function (e.g., a function defined on one or more database columns). A scoring function induces a unique total order on query results, where score ties are usually resolved using a deterministic tie-breaking criterion.

While most of the currently proposed ranking techniques focus on deterministic data, several emerging applications (e.g., Web mashups, location-based services, and sensor data management) involve data that are imprecise or uncertain. Dealing with data uncertainty by removing uncertain values is not desirable in many settings. For example, there could be too many uncertain values in the database (e.g., readings of sensing devices that become frequently unreliable under high temperature). Alternatively, there could be only few uncertain values in the database, but they are involved in data entities that closely match query requirements. Dropping such uncertain values may lead to inaccurate or incomplete query answers. For these reasons, modeling and processing uncertain data have been the focus of many recent studies [Benjelloun et al., 2006, Dalvi and Suciu, 2007, Sarma et al., 2006].

With data uncertainty, the semantics of ranking queries become unclear. For example, reporting a top ranked query result may not depend only on its computed score, but also on the potential uncertainty of that result as well as the scores and uncertainty of other query results. Ranking and uncertainty models interplay to determine meaningful interpretation of ranking queries in this context. We refer to this problem as the *Probabilistic Ranking Problem*.

In this lecture, we discuss the implications of two different types of data uncertainty on the semantics and processing techniques of ranking queries:

- *Tuple level uncertainty.* Tuples may belong to the database with less than absolute confidence. A widely-used model to capture this type of uncertainty is representing tuples as probabilistic events, and they model the database as a joint distribution defined on these events.

- *Attribute level uncertainty.* Tuple attributes may have uncertain values. A widely-used model to capture this type of uncertainty is representing tuple attributes as probability distributions defined on discrete or continuous domains.

This chapter starts by presenting real-world examples motivating the need for supporting ranking queries under tuple-level uncertainty (Section 1.1) and attribute-level uncertainty (Section 1.2). We then list the challenges raised by the integration of ranking and uncertainty models

Readings

	Time	Location	Make	PlateNo	Speed	Prob
t1	11:45	L1	Honda	X-123	130	0.4
t2	11:50	L1	Toyota	Y-245	120	0.7
t3	11:35	L2	Toyota	Y-245	80	0.3
t4	12:10	L3	Mazda	W-541	90	0.4
t5	12:25	L4	Mazda	W-541	110	0.6
t6	12:15	L4	Nissan	L-105	105	1.0

SELECT PlateNo, Make, Time
FROM Readings
WHERE Time BETWEEN '11:30' AND
'12:30'
ORDER BY Speed DESC
LIMIT _k_

(a)   (b)

Figure 1.1: (a) A relation with tuple uncertainty (b) Example ranking query

(Section 1.3). We finally present a classification of state-of-the-art probabilistic ranking techniques (Section 1.4).

1.1   TUPLE LEVEL UNCERTAINTY

We use the following example to illustrate the challenges involved in formulating and computing ranking queries under tuple level uncertainty:

Example 1.1   In a traffic-monitoring system, radars detect cars' speeds automatically, while car identification, e.g., by plate number, is performed by a human operator, or OCR of plate number images. In this system, multiple sources contribute to data uncertainty, e.g., high voltage lines that interfere with radars affecting their precision, close by cars that cannot be distinguished, or plate number images that are not clear enough to identify the car precisely. Figure 1.1(a) is a snapshot of speed Readings relation in the last hour. The special attribute "Prob" in each tuple indicates the probability that the whole tuple gives correct information. This probability can be obtained from various sources. For example, history of previous readings might indicate that 70% of the readings obtained from radars close to high voltage lines are actually correct. Hence, the readings of a radar unit that is close to high voltage lines can be assumed to be correct with probability 0.7. Other sources, e.g., clearness of plate number images, can be additionally incorporated to better quantify tuple's uncertainty.

Figure 1.1(b) shows an example ranking query to be evaluated on the Readings relation in Example 1.1. The given query is a Top-k Selection Query, in which scores are computed for base tuples, and the k query results with the highest scores are reported. The query requests the top-k speeding cars in one hour interval, which can be used, e.g., in an accident investigation scenario.

Although tuple scores (the *Speed* values) are given as deterministic values, the tuples themselves are uncertain. The *probabilities* and *scores* of tuples need to be factored in our interpretation of

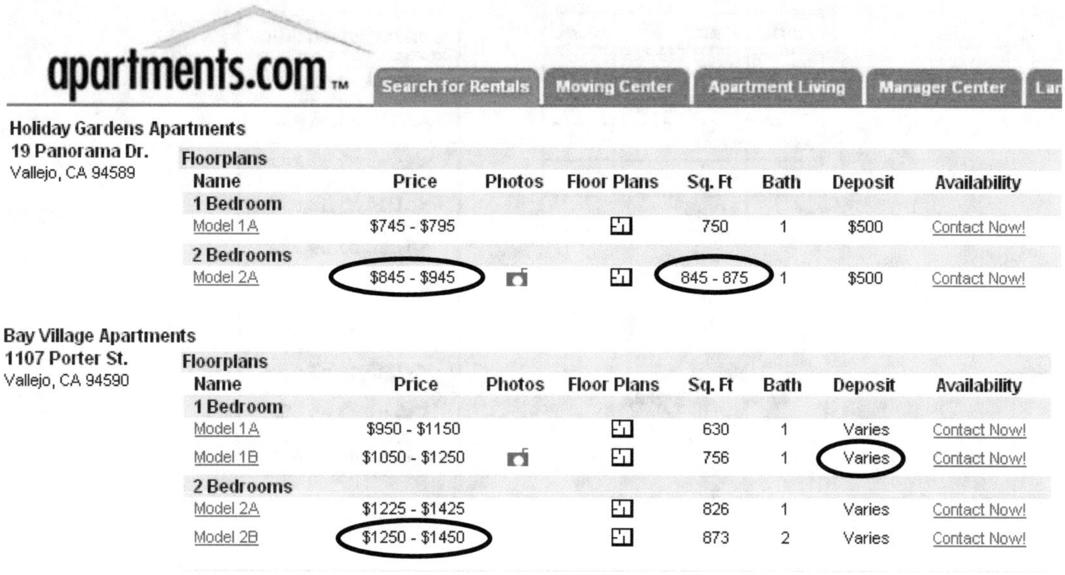
apartments.com™ Search for Rentals | Moving Center | Apartment Living | Manager Center | La

Holiday Gardens Apartments
19 Panorama Dr.
Vallejo, CA 94589

Floorplans

Name	Price	Photos	Floor Plans	Sq. Ft	Bath	Deposit	Availability
1 Bedroom							
Model 1A	$745 - $795			750	1	$500	Contact Now!
2 Bedrooms							
Model 2A	$845 - $945			845 - 875	1	$500	Contact Now!

Bay Village Apartments
1107 Porter St.
Vallejo, CA 94590

Floorplans

Name	Price	Photos	Floor Plans	Sq. Ft	Bath	Deposit	Availability
1 Bedroom							
Model 1A	$950 - $1150			630	1	Varies	Contact Now!
Model 1B	$1050 - $1250			756	1	Varies	Contact Now!
2 Bedrooms							
Model 2A	$1225 - $1425			826	1	Varies	Contact Now!
Model 2B	$1250 - $1450			873	2	Varies	Contact Now!

Figure 1.2: Uncertain data in search results

this query. This effectively introduces two interacting ranking dimensions that interplay to decide meaningful query answers. For example, it is not meaningful to report a top-scored tuple with insignificant probability. Moreover, combining scores and probabilities into one measure, using some aggregation function, eliminates uncertainty completely, and loses valuable information that can be used to get more meaningful answers conforming with probabilistic query models. We elaborate on this point in Section 3.2.

1.2 ATTRIBUTE LEVEL UNCERTAINTY

Uncertainty in attribute values induces uncertain scores when computing ranking queries. In contrast to conventional ranking settings, where a total order on query results is induced by the given scoring function, score uncertainty induces a *partial order* on the underlying tuples, where multiple rankings are valid.

To illustrate, consider Figure 1.2, which shows a snapshot of actual search results reported by `http://www.apartments.com` (accessed on December 28, 2010), for a simple search for available apartments to rent. The shown search results include several uncertain pieces of information. For example, some apartment listings do not explicitly specify the deposit amount. Other listings mention apartment rent and area as ranges rather than single values.

AptID	Rent	Score
a1	$600	9
a2	[$650-$1100]	[5-8]
a3	$800	7
a4	*negotiable*	[0-10]
a5	$1200	4

(a)

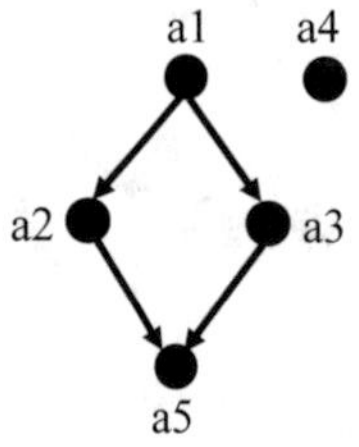

(b)

Linear Extensions
<a1,a4,a2,a3,a5>
<a1,a2,a3,a5,a4>
<a1,a3,a2,a5,a4>
<a1,a4,a3,a2,a5>
<a1,a2,a3,a4,a5>
<a1,a2,a4,a3,a5>
<a1,a3,a2,a4,a5>
<a1,a3,a4,a2,a5>
<a4,a1,a2,a3,a5>
<a4,a1,a3,a2,a5>

(c)

Figure 1.3: Partial order on tuples with uncertain scores

We illustrate the challenges involved in ranking with uncertain scores using the following simple example of the previous apartment search scenario.

Example 1.2   Assume an apartment database. Figure 1.3(a) gives a snapshot of the results of some query posed against such database. Assume that we are interested in ranking query results using a function that scores apartment records based on rent (the cheaper the apartment, the higher the score). Since the rent of apartment $a2$ is specified as a range, and the rent of apartment $a4$ is unknown, the scoring function assigns a range of possible scores to $a2$, while the full score range $[0 - 10]$ is assigned to $a4$.

Figure 1.3(b) depicts a diagram for the partial order induced by apartment scores. Disconnected nodes in the diagram indicate the incomparability of their corresponding records. Due to the intersection of score ranges, $a4$ is incomparable to all other records, and $a2$ is incomparable to $a3$.

A simple approach to compute a ranking based on the above partial order is to reduce it to a total order by replacing score ranges with their expected values. The problem with such approach, however, is that for score intervals with large variance, arbitrary rankings that are independent from how the ranges intersect may be produced. These rankings can be unreliable as we show in Chapter 3.

Another possible ranking query on partial orders is finding the skyline (i.e., the non-dominated objects [Chomicki, 2003]). An object is non-dominated if, in the partial order diagram, the object's node has no incoming edges. In Example 1.2, the skyline objects are $\{a1, a4\}$. The number of skyline objects can vary from a small number (e.g., Example 1.2) to the size of the whole database.

Furthermore, skyline objects may not be equally good and, similarly, dominated objects may not be equally bad. A user may want to compare objects' relative orders in different data exploration scenarios. Current proposals [Chan et al., 2006, Tao et al., 2007] have demonstrated that there is no unique way to distinguish or rank the skyline objects.

A different approach to rank the objects involved in a partial order is inspecting the space of possible rankings that conform to the relative order of objects. These rankings (or permutations) are called the *linear extensions* of the partial order. Figure 1.3(c) shows all linear extensions of the partial order in Figure 1.3(b). Inspecting the space of linear extensions allows ranking the objects in a way consistent with the partial order. For example, $a1$ may be preferred to $a4$ since $a1$ appears at rank 1 in 8 out of 10 linear extensions, even though both $a1$ and $a4$ are skyline objects. A crucial challenge for such approach is that the space of linear extensions grows exponentially in the number of objects [Brightwell and Winkler, 1991].

Furthermore, in many scenarios, uncertainty is quantified probabilistically. For example, a moving object's location can be described using a probability distribution defined on some region based on location history [Cheng et al., 2003]. Similarly, a missing attribute can be filled in with a probability distribution over possible predictions, using machine learning methods [Wolf et al., 2007]. Augmenting uncertain scores with such probabilistic quantifications generates a (possibly non-uniform) probability distribution of linear extensions that cannot be captured using a standard partial order or dominance relationship.

1.3 CHALLENGES

There are multiple challenges associated with incorporating data uncertainty in the semantics and processing techniques of top-k queries. We summarize such challenges as follows:

- *Query Semantics.* Proper semantics of top-k queries on uncertain data need to integrate the semantics of querying uncertain data with the conventional semantics of top-k queries. Different possible query semantics arise from this integration. For example, conventional top-k query semantics assume that each tuple has a single score and a distinct rank (by resolving ties using a deterministic tie breaker). However, under uncertainty, query semantics allowing for a range of possible scores per tuple, and hence a set of possible ranks per tuple, need to be adopted. This is a clear departure from the conventional semantics of top-k queries, and it is not also captured by current query semantics in uncertain databases.

- *Ranking Models.* Most current ranking models assume that computed tuple scores induce a total order on query results. Such a total order model is incapable of capturing uncertainty in the underlying data and its impact on the computed ranking of query results. While partial order models can capture uncertainty in the relative order of tuples, incorporating probabilistic ranking quantifications in such models requires new probabilistic modeling of partial orders. We thus need to construct new probabilistic ranking models different from the currently adopted ranking models.

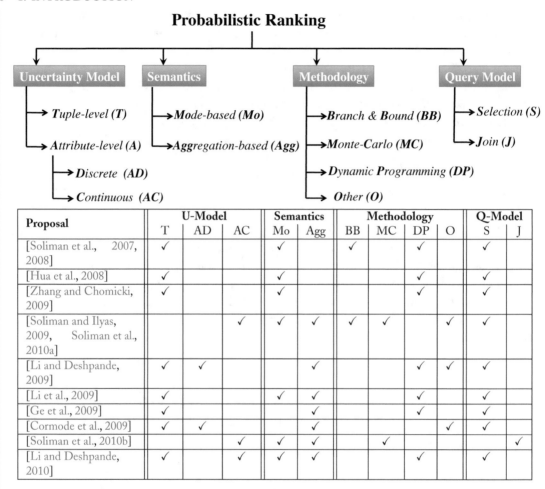

Probabilistic Ranking

Uncertainty Model
- Tuple-level (*T*)
- Attribute-level (*A*)
  - Discrete (*AD*)
  - Continuous (*AC*)

Semantics
- Mode-based (*Mo*)
- Aggregation-based (*Agg*)

Methodology
- Branch & Bound (*BB*)
- Monte-Carlo (*MC*)
- Dynamic Programming (*DP*)
- Other (*O*)

Query Model
- Selection (*S*)
- Join (*J*)

Proposal	U-Model			Semantics		Methodology				Q-Model	
	T	AD	AC	Mo	Agg	BB	MC	DP	O	S	J
[Soliman et al., 2007, 2008]	✓			✓		✓		✓		✓	
[Hua et al., 2008]	✓			✓				✓		✓	
[Zhang and Chomicki, 2009]	✓			✓				✓		✓	
[Soliman and Ilyas, 2009, Soliman et al., 2010a]			✓	✓	✓	✓	✓		✓	✓	
[Li and Deshpande, 2009]	✓	✓			✓			✓	✓	✓	
[Li et al., 2009]	✓			✓	✓			✓		✓	
[Ge et al., 2009]	✓				✓			✓		✓	
[Cormode et al., 2009]	✓	✓			✓				✓	✓	
[Soliman et al., 2010b]			✓	✓	✓	✓					✓
[Li and Deshpande, 2010]	✓		✓	✓	✓			✓		✓	

Figure 1.4: A classification of state-of-the-art probabilistic ranking techniques

- *Query Processing.* While minimizing the number of accessed tuples is central to most conventional ranking techniques, uncertainty adds further processing complexity, making existing methods inapplicable. Integrating ranking and uncertainty models yields a probability distribution over a huge space of possible rankings that is exponential in the database size. Hence, we need efficient algorithms to process such space in order to compute query answers. Under these settings, integrating tuple retrieval, ranking, and uncertainty management, within the same framework, is essential for efficient processing.

1.4   STATE-OF-THE-ART

The problem of probabilistic ranking has been first formulated by Soliman et al. [2007], who introduced the first query semantics and processing techniques of top-k queries on uncertain data. Later, multiple other proposals have introduced different problem formulations and query evaluation methods.

We present a high-level overview of state-of-the-art probabilistic ranking techniques. Figure 1.4 shows a taxonomy of current proposals. We discuss the major commonalities and differences among these proposals along four different dimensions:

1. *Uncertainty Model.* The impact of tuple-level and attribute-level uncertainty on probabilistic ranking has been addressed by current proposals from different perspectives. In most proposals, the two uncertainty types are handled in isolation by assuming that the database uncertainty model is either tuple-level or attribute-level. An important distinction among proposals that handle attribute-level uncertainty is their ability to support discrete and/or continuous domains of the uncertain attributes. For discrete uncertain attributes, a mapping can be constructed to model attribute-level uncertainty as tuple-level uncertainty, and hence leverage the ranking techniques developed for tuple-level uncertainty. Such mapping is not possible (without accuracy loss) when uncertain attributes have continuous domains. Consequently, specialized processing techniques that handle uncertainty in attributes with continuous domains have also been proposed.

   In Chapter 2, we describe in more detail the uncertainty models adopted by current probabilistic ranking techniques and the implications of the assumptions made by these models on ranking queries.

2. *Semantics.* The problem of probabilistic ranking entails processing and summarizing a probability distribution defined on a population of ranked instances of the underlying database. Motivated by the conventional practice of computing statistics (e.g., mean) to summarize a probability distribution, current proposals build on the definitions of two important statistics to formulate the semantics of ranking query answers:

   • Mode-based: Query answers are interpreted based on some probabilistic event that is most likely to occur in a random draw from the population of ranked instances. The definition of which event we are interested in monitoring is different among current proposals. For example, some proposals formulate the semantics of query answers based on the most likely prefix of ranked instances, while other proposals formulate the semantics based on the most likely individual tuples to appear at top ranks.

   • Aggregation-based: Query answers are interpreted based on an aggregation of the rankings given by the population of ranked instances. Two examples of these semantics are computing the expected rank of each tuple and finding a ranking that minimizes the disagreements among the possible ranked instances of the database.

In Chapter 3, we discuss proposed query semantics and their impact on the design of current probabilistic ranking proposals.

3. *Methodology.* The probabilistic ranking problem imposes non-trivial computational cost due to the need of processing/summarizing the distribution of ranked instances. A number of different methodologies and technical tools have been used and extended by current proposals to tackle the computational challenges of probabilistic ranking queries. These methodologies include branch-and-bound, Monte-Carlo simulation and dynamic programming techniques. In addition, a number of proposals have identified useful properties that can be exploited to devise other methods specific to the probabilistic ranking problem.

In Chapter 4, we describe in more detail the query evaluation methods introduced by current probabilistic ranking proposals. We categorize these methods based on their adopted approaches, and we discuss multiple examples under each category.

4. *Query Model.* Current probabilistic ranking proposals are mainly given under the Top-k Selection query model, in which scores are computed for base tuples retrieved from a single relation. Recent proposals extend such simplistic query model to handle more sophisticated ranking queries on uncertain databases. In particular, some proposals address probabilistic ranking under the Top-k Join query model, in which scores are computed for join results, rather than base tuples. The main challenge in handling relational operations, similar to join, in the context of probabilistic ranking, is that relational operations induce dependencies among the intermediate query results. Such dependencies need to be taken into consideration by the evaluation techniques of probabilistic ranking queries.

In Chapter 5, we describe in more detail how current proposals handle join queries in the context probabilistic ranking.

CHAPTER 2

Uncertainty Models

In this chapter, we give the details of a number of uncertainty models adopted by current probabilistic ranking proposals. In particular, we describe the impact of different aspects of tuple level (Section 2.1) and attribute level (Section 2.2) uncertainty models on the semantics and formulations of ranking queries.

2.1 TUPLE UNCERTAINTY MODELS

Under tuple uncertainty, tuples are represented as events, and the database is modeled as a joint distribution defined on these events. In order to formulate proper query semantics under such uncertainty model, many proposals [Abiteboul et al., 1987, Imieliński and Witold Lipski, 1984, Sarma et al., 2006] adopt *possible worlds* semantics, where a probabilistic database $\mathcal{D}$ is viewed as a set of possible instances (worlds). The possible worlds space represents an enumeration of all possible instances of the database, where each world is a subset of database tuples. The multiple possible instances of the database capture the uncertainty or incompleteness in the underlying data.

Possible worlds probabilities are determined based on the dependencies among tuples (e.g., mutual exclusion of tuples that map to the same real world entity [Sarma et al., 2006]). These dependencies are referred to as *generation rules* by Soliman et al. [2007, 2008] since they control how the possible worlds space is generated. Such rules could naturally arise with unclean data [Andritsos et al., 2006] or could be enforced to satisfy application requirements or reflect domain semantics [Benjelloun et al., 2006, Sarma et al., 2006]. Moreover, the relational processing of probabilistic tuples induces dependencies among intermediate query results even when base tuples are independent [Dalvi and Suciu, 2007]. We elaborate on this point in Chapter 5.

To illustrate, Figure 2.1(a) shows the Readings relation, from Example 1.1 in Chapter 1, augmented with *generation rules* that enforce the following requirement: "based on radar locations, the same car cannot be detected at two different locations within 1 hour interval." Figure 2.1(b) shows the possible worlds and their probabilities. Each world can be seen as a *joint* event of the *existence* of world's tuples and the *absence* of all other database tuples. The probability of this joint event is determined based on tuple probabilities and tuple dependencies. The given xor rules in Figure 2.1(a) mean that, in any possible world, the existence of $t2$ *implies* the absence of $t3$, and, similarly, the existence of $t4$ *implies* the absence of $t5$. All other tuples are independent. Consequently, $\Pr(\omega_1) = \Pr(t1 \wedge t2 \wedge t6 \wedge t4 \wedge \neg t3 \wedge \neg t5) = 0.4 \times 0.7 \times 1.0 \times 0.4 = 0.112$. The probabilities of other worlds are computed similarly. Any possible world, other than $\omega_1 \ldots \omega_8$, has zero probability based on tuple probabilities and generation rules.

	Time	Location	Make	PlateNo	Speed	Prob
t1	11:45	L1	Honda	X-123	130	0.4
t2	11:50	L1	Toyota	Y-245	120	0.7
t3	11:35	L2	Toyota	Y-245	80	0.3
t4	12:10	L3	Mazda	W-541	90	0.4
t5	12:25	L4	Mazda	W-541	110	0.6
t6	12:15	L4	Nissan	L-105	105	1.0

Generation Rules : $(t2 \oplus t3), (t4 \oplus t5)$

ω_1	ω_2	ω_3	ω_4
t1	t1	t1	t1
t2	t2	t6	t5
t6	t5	t4	t6
t4	t6	t3	t3
0.112	0.168	0.048	0.072

ω_5	ω_6	ω_7	ω_8
t2	t2	t6	t5
t6	t5	t4	t6
t4	t6	t3	t3
0.168	0.252	0.072	0.108

(a) **(b)**

Figure 2.1: Probabilistic database (a) Probabilistic relation and generation rules (b) Possible worlds space

As we show later in Chapter 3, some definitions of probabilistic ranking queries require computing the joint probability of a combination of tuple events. When all tuple events are independent, as in Figure 1.1, the joint probability of any combination of tuple events is computed by multiplying the probabilities of the corresponding tuple events. When tuple dependencies are captured by simple rules (e.g., implication or exclusiveness rules), the joint probability of any combination of tuple events is computed based on tuple probabilities and rules semantics. For example, for a rule $(t1 \oplus t2)$ that states that $t1$ is mutually exclusive with $t2$ (e.g., Figure 2.1), we have $\Pr(t1 \wedge t2) = 0$, while $\Pr(t1 \wedge \neg t2) = \Pr(t1)$. Similarly, for a rule $(t1 \rightarrow t2)$ that states that $t1$ implies $t2$, we have $\Pr(t1 \wedge t2) = \Pr(t1)$, while $\Pr(t1 \wedge \neg t2) = 0$. Similar types of rules have been used by Sen and Deshpande [2007] to capture tuple dependencies.

Uncertainty models supporting simple dependencies, similar to the above, are limited in their scope to special cases. A more general model is to maintain the explicit *joint probability distribution* of all database tuples. Factorization is a widely-adopted technique to decompose a complex joint distribution into a product of set of independent factors. Factorization techniques involve the use of factor graphs, where dependencies are maintained in the form of conditional probability tables exploiting the concept of conditional independence, and allowing representing arbitrary tuple dependencies.

Sen and Deshpande [2007] have introduced a graphical dependency model based on factor graphs. The model assumes Boolean variables associated with database tuples to capture their uncertain existence in the database. The modeled dependencies are represented as factors defined on the tuple random variables, where each factor enumerates the possible assignments of the tuples' variables dependent on a certain tuple t, as well as the conditional probability of t under each assignment. Each complete assignment of the tuple random variables gives one possible world (instance)

	Time	Location	Make	PlateNo	Speed	Prob
t1	11:45	L1	Honda	X-123	130	0.4
t2	11:50	L2	Toyota	Y-245	120	0.7
t3	11:35	L3	Toyota	Y-245	80	0.3
t4	12:10	L4	Mazda	W-541	90	0.4
t5	12:25	L5	Mazda	W-541	110	0.6
t6	12:15	L6	Nissan	L-105	105	1.0

World	Prob.
$\omega_1=\{t1,t2,t6,t4\}$	0.16
$\omega_2=\{t1,t2,t5,t6\}$	0.24
$\omega_3=\{t2,t6,t4\}$	0.12
$\omega_4=\{t2,t5,t6\}$	0.18
$\omega_5=\{t6,t4,t3\}$	0.12
$\omega_6=\{t5,t6,t4\}$	0.18

Generation Rules : $(t2 \oplus t3)$, $(t4 \oplus t5),(t1 \rightarrow t2)$

(a)   (b)

Figure 2.2: (a) Probabilistic relation (b) Possible Worlds

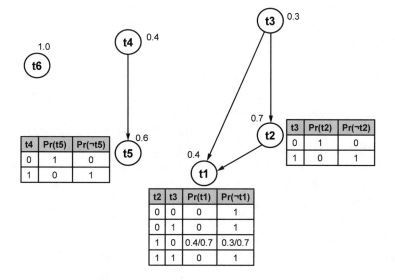

Figure 2.3: Factor graph

of the database. The probability of an instance is computed by multiplying all factors defined on the tuple random variables in the database.

We illustrate the model proposed by Sen and Deshpande [2007] using Figure 2.2, which shows the Readings relation augmented with mutual exclusion and implication dependencies. Figure 2.3 shows the corresponding factor graph that describe these dependencies. In the shown graph, connected tuples are conditionally dependent, while disconnected tuples are independent. Each tuple maintains a conditional probability table representing its conditional probability distribution given its parents. For example, the third row in the table of tuple $t1$ maintains the two conditional probabilities $Pr(t1|t2 \wedge \neg t3)$, and $Pr(\neg t1|t2 \wedge \neg t3)$. The dependencies and conditional probability tables are inferred from the semantics of the dependencies. However, this model is quite general since it can compactly encode arbitrary dependencies among tuple events. To illustrate, we show how to compute the joint probability $Pr(t1 \wedge t2 \wedge \neg t3)$. Based on Bayes chain rule, such joint probability is expressed as $Pr(\neg t3) \times Pr(t2|\neg t3) \times Pr(t1|t2 \wedge \neg t3) = 0.7 \times 1.0 \times \frac{0.4}{0.7} = 0.4$, which is the same as $Pr(t1)$ as implied by the semantics of the modeled dependencies.

Factor graphs have been also adopted by the uncertainty model proposed by Wick et al. [2010] to capture the dependencies among random variables corresponding to database objects such as tuples and attributes. In this model, the underlying relational database always represents a single world, and an external factor graph encodes a distribution over possible worlds. The given techniques combine the use of factor graphs with the MCMC method (discussed in Section 4.2.2) in order to provide scalable query evaluation. The MCMC method generates samples from the possible worlds space. The main idea is to evaluate the given query on deltas between consecutive samples generated by the MCMC method, rather than evaluate the query from scratch on each sample. The probability of a tuple t to be in the query answer is then approximated as the relative frequency of samples containing t.

Markov Logic Network (MLN) [Domingos and Lowd, 2009, Richardson and Domingos, 2006] is a related graphical dependency model that is based on integrating first order logic and Markov networks. Uncertainty in MLN is modeled as a set of first order logic formulas, each associated with a weight. Each formula expresses a constraint on the underlying data, while formula's weight expresses the strength of that constraint. Assigning a weight of ∞ to a formula F means that F is a hard constraint that should always hold, while assigning a finite weight to F means that F is a soft constraint that may be violated. We illustrate the previous model using Figure 2.4, which shows a simple example of Markov logic defined using two weighted first order formulas. The first formula models the uncertainty of the existence of data entities (for example, this can capture tuple uncertainty in an uncertain database), while the second formula models the exclusiveness of entities' existence (for example, this can capture generation rules given in Figure 2.1).

Let 'grounding' of a predicate p mean the assignment of variables in p to values from the corresponding domains. The grounding of a formula F means the grounding of all predicates involved in F. A Markov logic L can be represented graphically using a grounded MLN created by assigning each possible grounding of a predicate in L to a binary node, such that the value of that node is 1 if the ground predicate is true, and 0, otherwise. An edge is created between two nodes if the corresponding ground predicates appear together in at least one grounding of one formula in L. A possible world is given by assigning truth values to each grounded predicate in the graph.

We illustrate the previous graphical representation using Figure 2.4 where we assume the variables x and y range over a domain of three possible constants $\{t_1, t_2, t_3\}$. We further assume that only t_1 and t_2 are exclusive. Hence, we assign constant truth values to all the 'exclusive' nodes in the MLN, while the remaining 'exists' nodes are binary variables. Hence, the set of possible worlds contains 8 worlds created by taking all possible truth assignments of the three 'exists' variables. Given

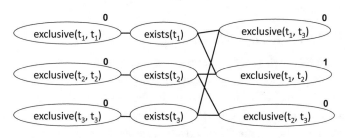

$$\forall x : exists(x) \qquad w_1$$
$$\forall x,y : exclusive(x,y) \Rightarrow (\neg x \vee \neg y) \qquad w_2$$

Markov Logic

Grounded Markov Network

Figure 2.4: Markov Logic Network

a Markov logic, where the weight of formula F_i is given by w_i, the probability of a possible world X is computed using the following log-linear model:

$$\Pr(X) = \frac{1}{Z} \cdot e^{\sum_{F_i} w_i \cdot n_i(X)}$$

where $n_i(X)$ is the number of true groundings of F_i in X, and Z is a normalizing constant computed as follows:

$$Z = \sum_{X \in \mathcal{X}} \prod_{F_i} e^{(w_i \cdot n_i(X))}$$

where $\mathcal{X}$ is the set of all possible worlds.

For example, in Figure 2.4, let the world $X = \{exists(t_1), exists(t_2), exists(t_3)\}$. Then, $\Pr(X) = e^{3w_1}/(e^{3w_1} + 3e^{(2w_1+w_2)} + 3e^{(w_1+w_2)} + e^{w_2})$, where the denominator is the normalizing constant Z. Hence, if we set $w_2 = \infty$, we get $\Pr(X) = 0$, since X violates the hard exclusiveness constraint between t_1 and t_2 in X. If, alternatively, we set w_2 to a finite value, the value of $\Pr(X)$ will be inversely proportional to w_2, since X violates a soft constraint in this case.

2.2   ATTRIBUTE UNCERTAINTY MODELS

When the values of one or more uncertain attributes are used to compute tuple scores in ranking queries, the resulting scores become uncertain. We are interested in modeling the impact of uncertain scores on the semantics and processing of ranking queries. In general, there are two types of score uncertainty: *discrete* and *continuous*. In discrete score uncertainty, each tuple has a finite set of possible scores each associated with a probability value. In continuous score uncertainty, tuple's score is modeled as a probability distribution defined on a continuous range of possible scores. In the following sections, we describe the details of both models and give example proposals under each model.

2.2.1   DISCRETE UNCERTAIN SCORES

Under attribute uncertainty in discrete domains, tuple's score is modeled as a probability distribution defined on a finite set of possible scores. For example, assume that PlateNo is a key in the `Readings` relation in Figure 2.1. Figure 2.5 shows a version of the `Readings` relation complying with such key constraint, where each set of tuples with identical keys are coalesced into the same tuple. Under discrete score uncertainty, each tuple is effectively a group of identical tuple instances, and each instance is assigned a different score. The uncertainty in tuple scores can be mapped to tuple uncertainty by transforming the relation with discrete attribute uncertainty into its 1NF, as shown in Figure 2.5. The exclusiveness rules enforce that no two instances of the same tuple co-exist in the same possible world. Note that this transformation is only possible for discrete score distributions, since for continuous score distribution, there is an infinite number of possible instances per tuple. The transformation also has clear scalability issues for large discrete score distributions.

An important distinction between the previous mapping and the original tuple uncertainty model is that the occurrences of different instances of a tuple r in possible worlds need to be aggregated since they represent different ranking possibilities of the same source tuple r. Such a requirement does not exist in the original tuple uncertainty model where each tuple acts as a standalone entity.

The and/xor tree model proposed by Li and Deshpande [2009] captures mutual exclusion/co-existence dependencies in a tree structure, allowing for combining tuple uncertainty and discrete attribute uncertainty under the same model.

Definition 2.1   [And/Xor Tree] [Li and Deshpande, 2009] A tree where each leaf node is a tuple instance, and each internal node is labeled with either ($\vee$) or ($\wedge$). The edge connecting a ($\vee$) node u to one of its children v is labeled with a non-negative value $P_{u,v}$ such that $\sum_{v \in children(u)} P_{u,v} \leq 1$. The edges between a ($\wedge$) node and its children are unlabeled. Moreover, the least common ancestor of any two leaf nodes, corresponding to the same source tuple, must be a ($\vee$) node.   □

Given a node u, the and/xor tree model inductively defines a possible world ω_u (a subset of the leaves of the subtree rooted by u) by the following recursive process:

- If u is a leaf, $\omega_u = \{u\}$.

- If u is a ($\vee$) node, $\omega_u = \begin{cases} \omega_v & with\ probability\ P_{u,v} \\ \phi & with\ probability\ 1 - \sum_{v \in children(u)} P_{u,v} \end{cases}$

		PlateNo	Speed
r1	...	X-123	{130:0.4}
r2	...	Y-245	{120:0.7, 80:0.3}
r3	...	W-541	{90:0.4, 110:0.6}
r4	...	L-105	{105:1.0}

Readings relation where PK is **PlateNo**

		PlateNo	Speed	Prob
r1.1	...	X-123	130	0.4
r2.1	...	Y-245	120	0.7
r2.2	...	Y-245	80	0.3
r3.1	...	W-541	90	0.4
r3.2	...	W-541	110	0.6
r4.1	...	L-105	105	1.0

$(r2.1 \oplus r2.2), (r3.1 \oplus r3.2)$

An equivalent relation under tuple
uncertainty model

Figure 2.5: Mapping discrete attribute uncertainty to tuple uncertainty

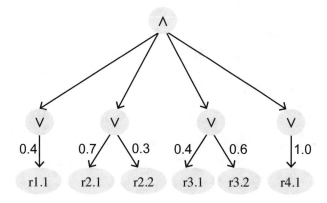

Figure 2.6: An equivalent And/xor tree model [Li and Deshpande, 2009]

- If u is a ($\wedge$) node, $\omega_u = \bigcup_{v \in children(u)} \omega_v$.

For example, Figure 2.6 shows the and/xor tree corresponding to the relation shown in Figure 2.5.

The and/xor tree model compactly encodes the distribution of tuples over different ranks based on the notion of *generating functions*, discussed in Section 4.3.2.

2.2.2   CONTINUOUS UNCERTAIN SCORES

Under attribute uncertainty in continuous domains, tuple's score is a continuous real range associated with a probability density function capturing the likelihood of possible score values. Formally, the score of tuple t_i is modeled as a probability density function f_i defined on a real score interval $[lo_i, up_i]$, where lo_i is the score lower-bound of t_i and up_i is the score upper-bound of t_i. Figure 2.7

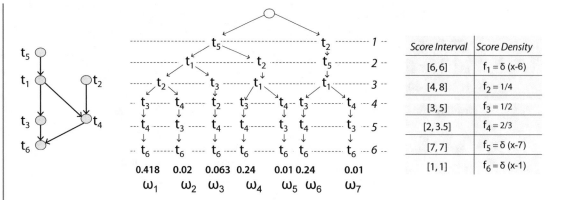

Figure 2.7: Modeling score uncertainty [Soliman and Ilyas, 2009]

shows a set of tuples with uniform score densities, where $f_i = 1/(up_i - lo_i)$ (e.g., $f_2 = 1/4$). For tuples with deterministic scores (e.g., t_1), we have an impulse density $f_i = \delta(x - lo_i)$ (effectively, the score density of a tuple t_i with a deterministic score is an impulse function with infinite value at $x = lo_i$ or, equivalently, at $x = up_i$).

Based on the previous simple model, Soliman and Ilyas [2009], Soliman et al. [2010a] have proposed capturing uncertain continuous scores using a probabilistic partial order that extends the following definition of *strict partial order*:

Definition 2.2   [Strict Partial Order] A strict partial order $\mathbb{P}$ is a 2-tuple $(\mathcal{R}, \mathcal{O})$, where $\mathcal{R}$ is a finite set of elements, and $\mathcal{O} \subset \mathcal{R} \times \mathcal{R}$ is a binary relation with the following properties:
(1) Non-reflexivity: $\forall i \in \mathcal{R} : (i, i) \notin \mathcal{O}$.
(2) Asymmetry: If $(i, j) \in \mathcal{O}$, then $(j, i) \notin \mathcal{O}$.
(3) Transitivity: If $\{(i, j), (j, k)\} \subset \mathcal{O}$, then $(j, k) \in \mathcal{O}$.   □

Strict partial orders allow the relative order of some elements to be left undefined. A widely-used depiction of partial orders is Hasse diagram (e.g., Figure 1.3(b)), which is a DAG whose nodes are the elements of $\mathcal{R}$, and edges are the binary relationships in $\mathcal{O}$, except relationships derived by transitivity. An edge (i, j) indicates that i is ranked above j according to $\mathbb{P}$. The *linear extensions* of a partial order are all possible topological sorts of the partial order graph (i.e., the relative order of any two elements in any linear extension does not violate the set of binary relationships $\mathcal{O}$).

The model proposed by Soliman and Ilyas [2009] extends strict partial orders to encode score uncertainty. We define the notion of *score dominance* as follows: A tuple t_i *dominates* another tuple t_j iff $lo_i \geq up_j$ (i.e., the score lower-bound of t_i is not below the score upper-bound of t_j). The deterministic tie-breaker τ eliminates cycles when applying score dominance to tuples with deterministic equal scores. It immediately follows that Score Dominance is a *non-reflexive*, *asymmetric* and *transitive* relation.

By assuming the independence of score densities of individual tuples, the probability that tuple t_i is ranked above tuple t_j, denoted $\Pr(t_i > t_j)$, is given by the following 2-dimensional integral:

$$\Pr(t_i > t_j) = \int_{lo_i}^{up_i} \int_{lo_j}^{x} f_i(x) \cdot f_j(y) dy\, dx \qquad (2.1)$$

When neither t_i nor t_j dominates the other tuple, $[lo_i, up_i]$ and $[lo_j, up_j]$ are intersecting intervals, and so $\Pr(t_i > t_j)$ belongs to the open interval $(0, 1)$, and $\Pr(t_j > t_i) = 1 - \Pr(t_i > t_j)$. On the other hand, if t_i dominates t_j, then we have $\Pr(t_i > t_j) = 1$ and $P(t_j > t_i) = 0$. We say that a tuple pair (t_i, t_j) belongs to a *probabilistic dominance relation* iff $\Pr(t_i > t_j) \in (0, 1)$. We next give the formal definition of the probabilistic ranking model given by Soliman and Ilyas [2009].

Definition 2.3   [Probabilistic Partial Order (PPO)] [Soliman and Ilyas, 2009] Let $\mathcal{R} = \{t_1, \ldots, t_n\}$ be a set of real intervals, where each interval $t_i = [lo_i, up_i]$ is associated with a density function f_i such that $\int_{lo_i}^{up_i} f_i(x) dx = 1$. The set $\mathcal{R}$ induces a probabilistic partial order PPO$(\mathcal{R}, \mathcal{O}, \mathcal{P})$, where $(\mathcal{R}, \mathcal{O})$ is a strict partial order with $(t_i, t_j) \in \mathcal{O}$ iff t_i dominates t_j. Moreover, $\mathcal{P}$ is the *probabilistic dominance relation* of intervals in $\mathcal{R}$.   □

Definition 2.3 states that if t_i dominates t_j, then $(t_i, t_j) \in \mathcal{O}$. That is, we can deterministically rank t_i above t_j. On the other hand, if neither t_i nor t_j dominates the other tuple, then $(t_i, t_j) \in \mathcal{P}$. That is, the uncertainty in the relative order of t_i and t_j is quantified by $\Pr(t_i > t_j)$.

Figure 2.7 shows the Hasse diagram of the PPO of the shown tuples, as well as the set of linear extensions of the PPO.

The linear extensions of PPO$(\mathcal{R}, \mathcal{O}, \mathcal{P})$ can be viewed as tree where each root-to-leaf path is one linear extension. The root node is a dummy node since there can be multiple elements in $\mathcal{R}$ that may be ranked first. Each occurrence of an element $t \in \mathcal{R}$ in the tree represents a possible ranking of t, and each level i in the tree contains all elements that occur at rank i in any linear extension.

Score dominance allows computing a rank interval for each tuple, defined as follows:

Definition 2.4   [Rank Interval] The rank interval of a tuple t is the range of all possible ranks of t in the linear extensions of the PPO.   □

For a relation R of size n and a tuple $t \in R$, let $U(t)$ and $L(t)$ be the tuple subsets in R dominating t and dominated by t, respectively. Then, the rank interval of t is given by $[|U(t)| + 1, n - |L(t)|]$. For example, in Figure 2.7 for t_5, we have $U(t_5) = \phi$, and $L(t_5) = \{t_1, t_3, t_4, t_6\}$, and thus the rank interval of t_5 is $[1, 2]$.

Due to probabilistic dominance, the space of possible linear extensions is viewed as a probability space generated by a probabilistic process that draws, for each tuple t_i, a random score

$s_i \in [lo_i, up_i]$ based on the density f_i. Ranking the drawn scores gives a total order on the database tuples, where the probability of such order is the joint probability of the drawn scores. For example, we show in Figure 2.7, the probability value associated with each linear extension. We show next how to compute these probabilities.

The PPO model allows for formulating a probability space over the set of possible tuple orderings, given by the linear extensions. The probability of a linear extension is computed as a nested integral over tuples' score densities in the order given by the linear extension. Let $\omega = \langle t_1, t_2, \ldots t_n \rangle$ be a linear extension. Then, $\Pr(\omega)$ is given by the following n-dimensional integral with dependent limits:

$$\Pr(\omega) = \int_{lo_1}^{up_1} \int_{lo_2}^{x_1} \cdots \int_{lo_n}^{x_{n-1}} f_1(x_1) \ldots f_n(x_n) dx_n \ldots dx_1 \tag{2.2}$$

Monte-Carlo integration can be used to compute complex nested integrals such as Equation 2.2. For example, the probabilities of linear extensions $\omega_1, \ldots, \omega_7$ in Figure 2.7 are computed using the Monte-Carlo integration method described in the following.

Monte-Carlo Integration.   The method of Monte-Carlo integration [O'Leary, 2004] computes accurate estimate of the integral $\int_{\acute{\Gamma}} f(x) dx$, where $\acute{\Gamma}$ is an arbitrary volume, by sampling from another volume $\Gamma \supseteq \acute{\Gamma}$ in which uniform sampling and volume computation are easy. The volume $\acute{\Gamma}$ is estimated as the proportion of samples from Γ that are inside $\acute{\Gamma}$ multiplied by the volume of Γ. The average $f(x)$ over such samples is used to compute the integral. Specifically, let v be the volume of Γ, s be the total number of samples, and $x_1 \ldots x_m$ be the samples that are inside $\acute{\Gamma}$. Then, the value of the integral can be estimated as follows:

$$\int_{\acute{\Gamma}} f(x) dx \approx \frac{m}{s} \cdot v \cdot \frac{1}{m} \sum_{i=1}^{m} f(x_i) \tag{2.3}$$

In general, let Γ be a sample space in which uniform independent sampling can be done. Assume that we would like to estimate ρ, the volume of some subspace embedded in Γ relative to the volume of Γ. Given two real numbers $\epsilon \in (0, 1]$ and $\delta \in (0, 1]$, the Monte-Carlo method computes an estimate of ρ, denoted $\hat{\rho}$, such that $\Pr(\, |\rho - \hat{\rho}| \leq \epsilon \cdot \rho) \geq (1 - \delta)$, provided that the number of drawn samples from Γ is in $\Omega(\frac{1}{\rho \cdot \epsilon^2} ln(\frac{1}{\delta}))$ [Motwani and Raghavan, 1997].

CHAPTER 3

Query Semantics

In this chapter, we present different proposed semantics of top-k queries on uncertain data. We abstract the details of the uncertainty model (which can be either tuple-level or attribute-level uncertainty model) by formulating query semantics on a finite set of possible worlds $\mathcal{W} = \{\omega_1, \ldots, \omega_n\}$, where each world $\omega_i \in \mathcal{W}$ is a valid ranked instance of the database. We denote with $\omega_i(t)$ the rank/position of tuple t in ω_i. We elaborate on the ranking requirement of worlds in $\mathcal{W}$, using the example given by Figure 3.1.

Under tuple level uncertainty, each world $\omega_i \in \mathcal{W}$ is a subset of database tuples ranked based on the scores given by a query-specified scoring function. For example, Figure 3.1(a) shows the possible worlds of the Readings relation in Figure 2.1, ranked on the *Speed* attribute.

Under attribute level uncertainty, each world $\omega_i \in \mathcal{W}$ is a permutation of all database tuples corresponding to a possible linear extension of the PPO induced by uncertain scores. For example, Figure 3.1(b) shows the ranked possible worlds (linear extensions) of the PPO in Figure 2.7.

In the following, for two tuples t_i and t_j, we denote with $(t_i > t_j)$ the preference of t_i over t_j in the computed ranking of query results. Under tuple level uncertainty, for two tuples t_i and t_j, where $score(t_i) > score(t_j)$, we have $(t_i > t_j)$ in all ranked possible worlds containing both t_i and t_j. On the other hand, under attribute level uncertainty, if $score(t_i)$ dominates $score(t_j)$ (i.e., the lowest score of t_i is $\geq$ the highest score of t_j), then $(t_i > t_j)$ in all ranked possible worlds. Otherwise, $(t_i > t_j)$ in a subset of possible worlds, while $(t_j > t_i)$ in the remaining possible worlds.

The proposed semantics of probabilistic ranking queries build on possible worlds semantics, where we obtain the probability of a query answer by aggregating the probabilities of possible worlds supporting that answer. Intuitively, we would like to obtain answers that are strongly supported in the space of possible answers. In general, proposed probabilistic ranking semantics can be classified into two main groups: *mode-based* semantics, where the computed ranking is (with high probability) the ranking obtained from a random possible world, and *aggregation-based* semantics, where the computed ranking is an aggregation of the rankings defined by different possible worlds.

3.1 MODE-BASED SEMANTICS

Mode-based query semantics assume a randomized process that picks a random possible world, and it evaluates a top-k query on this world. The goal is to return the answer which will most likely be reported by this process.

An orthogonal construct to the previous formulation is answer's granularity. We project the space of possible worlds on different dimensions representing granularity levels, namely, tuple vectors,

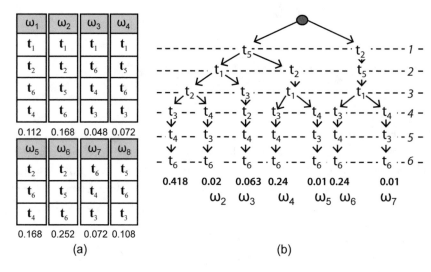

Figure 3.1: Ranked possible worlds under (a) tuple uncertainty (b) attribute uncertainty

tuple sets, tuples appearing in a range of ranks, and full tuple orderings. Answering ranking queries at these different granularity levels can be useful to a wide class of applications, as we show at the end of this chapter.

The input to each of the following query definitions is the set of ranked possible worlds represented as orderings of tuple IDs, while the output is a sequence/set of tuple IDs satisfying a given condition.

Definition 3.1   [Uncertain Top Prefix (UTop-Prefix)] [Soliman and Ilyas, 2009, Soliman et al., 2007] A UTop-Prefix(k) query returns the most probable vector of top-k tuples. That is, UTop-Prefix(k) returns $argmax_p(\sum_{\omega \in W_{(p,k)}} \Pr(\omega))$, where $W_{(p,k)} \subseteq \mathcal{W}$ is the set of possible worlds having p as the k-length prefix.   □

UTop-Prefix query returns the tuple vector with the highest probability of being the top-k vector across all worlds. That is, UTop-Prefix query answer is the mode of the distribution of possible top-k answers. For example, in Figure 3.1(a), a UTop-Prefix(2) query returns $\langle t_1, t_2 \rangle$ with probability 0.28 since $\langle t_1, t_2 \rangle$ is the top-2 vector in ω_1 and ω_2 whose probability summation is 0.28, which is the maximum probability among all possible top-2 vectors. Similarly, in Figure 3.1(b), a UTop-Prefix(3) query returns $\langle t_5, t_1, t_2 \rangle$ with probability $\Pr(\omega_1) + \Pr(\omega_2) = 0.438$.

Definition 3.2   [Uncertain Top Set (UTop-Set)][Soliman and Ilyas, 2009] A UTop-Set(k) query returns the most probable set of top-k tuples. That is, UTop-Set(k) returns

$argmax_s(\sum_{\omega \in W_{(s,k)}} Pr(w))$, where $W_{(s,k)} \subseteq W$ is the set of possible worlds having s as the set of top-k tuples. $\square$

Unlike UTop-Prefix query, UTop-Set query ignores the order of tuples within query answer (i.e., how should tuples be ordered in the reported answer). However, UTop-Set and UTop-Prefix query answers are related since the top-k set probability of a set s is the summation of the top-k prefix probabilities of all prefixes p that consist of the same tuples of s. Under tuple level uncertainty, the relative order of any two tuples is fixed across all possible worlds, and hence UTop-Set and UTop-Prefix queries return identical answers. On the other hand, under attribute level uncertainty, UTop-Set and UTop-Prefix query answers are not necessarily identical.

For example, in Figure 3.1(a), a UTop-Set(2) query returns $\{t_1, t_2\}$ with probability 0.28, which is the same as UTop-Prefix(2) query answer. On the other hand, in Figure 3.1(b), the query UTop-Set(3) returns the set $\{t_1, t_2, t_5\}$ with probability $Pr(\omega_1) + Pr(\omega_2) + Pr(\omega_4) + Pr(\omega_5) + Pr(\omega_6) + Pr(\omega_7) = 0.937$. Note that $\{t_1, t_2, t_5\}$ appears as Prefix $\langle t_5, t_1, t_2 \rangle$ in ω_1 and ω_2, appears as Prefix $\langle t_5, t_2, t_1 \rangle$ in ω_4 and ω_5, and appears as Prefix $\langle t_2, t_5, t_1 \rangle$ in ω_6 and ω_7.

Definition 3.3   [Uncertain Top Rank (UTop-Rank)][Soliman and Ilyas, 2009] A UTop-Rank(i, j) query, for $i \leq j$, returns the most probable tuple to appear at any rank $i \ldots j$ (i.e., from i to j inclusive) in possible worlds in W. That is, UTop-Rank(i, j) returns $argmax_t(\sum_{\omega \in W_{(t,i,j)}} Pr(\omega))$, where $W_{(t,i,j)} \subseteq W$ is the set of possible worlds with the tuple t at any rank $i \ldots j$. $\square$

UTop-Rank query returns the tuple that appears in a given range of ranks with the highest probability. For example, in Figure 3.1(a), a UTop-Rank(1, 2) query answer is t_2 with probability 0.7, since t_2 appears at rank 1 in ω_5 and ω_6, and appears at rank 2 in ω_1 and ω_2, where $Pr(\omega 1) + Pr(\omega_2) + Pr(\omega_5) + Pr(\omega_6) = 0.7$. Similarly, in Figure 3.1(b), a UTop-Rank(1, 2) query returns t_5 with probability $Pr(\omega_1) + \cdots + Pr(\omega_7) = 1.0$, since t_5 appears at all linear extensions at either rank 1 or rank 2. It also follows from possible worlds semantics that UTop-Rank(i, j) probability of a tuple t is the summation of the UTop-Rank(r, r) probabilities of t for $r = i \ldots j$.

The previous definition of UTop-Rank query is a generalization of the definition of U-k Ranks query given by Soliman et al. [2007], where the objective is reporting the most probable tuple to appear at each rank $1 \ldots k$. Two other proposed query semantics can be formulated as variations of UTop-Rank query. The first query semantics is Global Top-k query [Zhang and Chomicki, 2009], which returns the k most probable tuples to appear at any rank $1 \ldots k$ (which is the same as finding the k tuples maximizing UTop-Rank$(1, k)$ probabilities). The second query semantics is Probabilistic Threshold top-k (PT-k) query [Hua et al., 2008], which, given a threshold T, returns all tuples whose probabilities of appearing at any rank $1 \ldots k$ are $\geq T$ (which is the same as finding all tuples whose UTop-Rank$(1, k)$ probabilities are at least T).

The previous query definitions can be extended to rank different answers on probability. We define the answer of l-UTop-Prefix(k) query as the l most probable prefixes of length k. We define the answer of l-UTop-Set(k) query as the l most probable top-k sets. We define the answer of l-UTop-Rank(i, j) query as the l most probable tuples to appear at a rank $i \ldots j$. We assume a tie-breaker that deterministically orders answers with equal probabilities.

3.2   AGGREGATION-BASED SEMANTICS

An intuitive and simple choice of aggregation-based probabilistic ranking semantics is ranking the tuples based on their expected scores. We show in the next two examples that such a simple approach can result in unreliable rankings under both tuple level and attribute level uncertainty models.

Example 3.4   *Expected Scores under Tuple Uncertainty.* Assume 2 tuples t_1 and t_2, where $score(t_1) = 1000$, $score(t_2) = 1$, $\Pr(t_1) = 0.01$, and $\Pr(t_2) = 1$. Then, the expected scores of t_1 and t_2 are 10 and 1, respectively. The ranking based on expected scores is thus $\langle t_1, t_2 \rangle$. That is , t_1 is ranked first even though $\Pr(t_1)$ is very low. Moreover, if $score(t_1)$ drops to 10, the ranking becomes $\langle t_2, t_1 \rangle$. That is, the ranks of t_1 and t_2 are reversed even though $score(t_1) > score(t_2)$ in both cases.

Example 3.5   *Expected Scores under Attribute Uncertainty.* Assume 3 tuples, t_1, t_2, and t_3 with score intervals [0, 100], [40, 60], and [30, 70], respectively. Assume that score values are distributed uniformly within each interval. The expected score of each tuple is thus 50, and hence all permutations are equally likely rankings. However, as we show in Section 2.2, we can compute the probabilities of different rankings of these tuples as follows: $\Pr(\langle t_1, t_2, t_3 \rangle) = 0.25$, $\Pr(\langle t_1, t_3, t_2 \rangle) = 0.2$, $\Pr(\langle t_2, t_1, t_3 \rangle) = 0.05$, $\Pr(\langle t_2, t_3, t_1 \rangle) = 0.2$, $\Pr(\langle t_3, t_1, t_2 \rangle) = 0.05$, and $\Pr(\langle t_3, t_2, t_1 \rangle) = 0.25$. That is, the rankings have a non-uniform distribution even though the score intervals are uniform with equal expectations.

The two previous examples illustrate that the dimensions of scores and probabilities need to be aggregated in a different way to comply with the semantics of both dimensions, and produce meaningful ranking. In the following, we discuss a group of aggregation-based ranking semantics that are formulated by defining an aggregation on the rankings given by different possible worlds.

Expected Ranks. The first aggregation-based query semantics we discuss is *expected ranks* [Cormode et al., 2009], which ranks tuples based on their expected ranks. Given an ordering of tuples ω, let $\omega(t)$ denote the rank (position) of a tuple t in ω. The expected rank is defined as follows:

Definition 3.6   **[Expected Rank (ER)][**Cormode et al., 2009**]** An ER query returns an ordering of tuples based on their expected ranks in the distribution of ranked possible worlds. The rank of tuple t in a ranked possible world ω is given by

$$r_\omega(t) = \begin{cases} |\{t' | \omega(t') < \omega(t)\}| & if \ t \in \omega \\ |\omega| & otherwise \end{cases}.$$

The expected rank of t is defined as $ER(t) = \sum_{\omega \in \mathcal{W}} \Pr(\omega) * r_\omega(t)$.   □

For example, in Figure 3.1(a), $ER(t_1) = 0.4 * 0 + 0.6 * 3 = 1.8$, since t_1 appears at rank 1 in $\omega_1 \ldots \omega_4$ whose probability summation is 0.4, while t_1 does not exist in $\omega_5 \ldots \omega_8$ whose probability summation is 0.6, and the size of each world is 3. The ordering of all tuples in Figure 3.1(a) based on expected ranks gives $\langle t_2 : 1.3, t_6 : 1.7, t_1 : 1.8, t_5 : 2.02, t_4 : 2.88, t_3 : 3.1 \rangle$

Cormode et al. [2009] have formulated a number of plausible properties of the semantics of ranking queries:

- Exact-k: A top-k answer contains exactly k tuples.

- Containment: The top-$(k + 1)$ answer contains the top-k answer.

- Unique ranking: Each tuple appears in a unique position in the top-k answer.

- Value invariance: Changing the scores of tuples without changing their relative order should not alter the top-k answer.

- Stability: If tuple t is part of the top-k answer, then t should remain in the top-k answer if its score is increased.

Cormode et al. [2009] have shown that the previous properties are maintained under expected ranks, while they are partially maintained by mode-based semantics. However, adopting expected ranks semantics can be problematic in other cases. For example, similar to other expectation-based statistics, expected ranks can be easily thrown off with the existence of outliers. This means that we might not be able to report tuples with very high scores and probabilities if the majority of other tuples have low scores and/or probabilities. This is not the case with mode-based semantics that do not rely on computing expected values. Hence, there is a need for supporting both mode-based and aggregation-based semantics in order to handle probabilistic ranking queries in a wider range of applications and data distributions.

Uncertain Rank Aggregation. The second query semantics we discuss is URank-Agg [Li and Deshpande, 2009, Soliman and Ilyas, 2009, Soliman et al., 2010a], which treats possible worlds as voters whose opinions regarding the ranking of tuples need to be aggregated to compute the output ranking.

Definition 3.7   [Uncertain Rank Aggregation Query (URank-Agg)][Li and Deshpande, 2009, Soliman and Ilyas, 2009, Soliman et al., 2010a] A URank-Agg query returns a tuple ordering ω^* that minimizes $\sum_{\omega \in \mathcal{W}} \Pr(\omega) \cdot d(\omega^*, \omega)$, where $d(.,.)$ is a measure of the distance between two orderings.   □

URank-Agg query returns a consensus ordering that has the minimum average distance to all ranked possible worlds. The definition of URank-Agg query involves a function d that measures the distance between two ordered lists (ranked worlds). The most common definitions of such functions assume orderings of exactly the same set of elements. Two widely used distance functions are the Spearman footrule distance and the Kendall tau distance.

The Spearman footrule distance is the summation, over all tuples, of the distance between the positions of the same tuple in the two lists, formally defined as follows:

$$F(\omega_i, \omega_j) = \sum_t |\omega_i(t) - \omega_j(t)| \qquad (3.1)$$

where $\omega(t)$ denotes the rank of tuple t in the ordering ω.

On the other hand, the Kendall tau distance is the number of pairwise disagreements in the relative order of tuples in the two lists, formally defined as follows:

$$K(\omega_i, \omega_j) = |\{(t_a, t_b) : a < b, \ \omega_i(t_a) < \omega_i(t_b), \omega_j(t_a) > \omega_j(t_b)\}| \qquad (3.2)$$

These two distance functions apply only to attribute-level uncertainty model since the ranked possible worlds under such model are permutations of all database tuples [Soliman and Ilyas, 2009, Soliman et al., 2010a]. On the other hand, under tuple level uncertainty, the possible worlds may involve different subsets of database tuples, which requires adopting a different distance function that applies to partial lists. Computing distance between partial lists has been addressed by Fagin et al. [2003] where variations of the Spearman footrule and Kendall tau distance functions, as well as other distance functions, are proposed to allow computing optimal aggregation on partial lists.

Li and Deshpande [2009] considered three of the distance functions proposed by Fagin et al. [2003] to find a consensus top-k ranking. Let τ be a top-k list, and τ^n, for $1 \leq n \leq k$, be the n-length prefix in τ. Let $\sigma^l(t, \tau)$ be a function defined as $\sigma_i^l(t, \tau) = \tau(t)$ if $t \in \tau$, and $\sigma_i^l(t, \tau) = l$, otherwise. Given two top-k lists τ_i and τ_j (in general, τ_i and τ_j may not contain the same set of tuples), the distance between τ_i and τ_j is given by one of the following functions:

- Symmetric Difference:
$$\Delta(\tau_i, \tau_j) = |(\tau_i \setminus \tau_j) \cup (\tau_j \setminus \tau_i)| \qquad (3.3)$$

- Intersection:
$$I(\tau_i, \tau_j) = \frac{1}{k} \sum_{n=1}^{k} \Delta(\tau_i^n, \tau_j^n) \qquad (3.4)$$

- Extended Footrule:
$$F^{(l)}(\tau_i, \tau_j) = \sum_t |\sigma^l(t, \tau_i) - \sigma^l(t, \tau_j)| \qquad (3.5)$$

Figure 3.2 shows the distance between two lists, τ_i and τ_j, as well as the distance between the top-2 partial lists of τ_i and τ_j, according to the previous distance functions. For example, we show how we compute $F^{(3)}(\tau_i^2, \tau_j^2)$. We iterate over tuples in the order given by τ_i, resulting in $F^{(3)}(\tau_i^2, \tau_j^2) = |1 - 2| + |2 - 3| + |3 - 1| + |3 - 3| + |3 - 3| + |3 - 3| = 4$.

Typical Top-k. The third query semantics we discuss is Typical Top-k Vectors [Ge et al., 2009], which extends the semantics of UTop-Prefix by adopting an expectation-based approach. The semantics of UTop-Prefix query defines top-k query answer as the mode of the probability distribution of k-length prefixes in ranked possible worlds (k-prefixes for short). Let p^* be probability of the k-prefix reported by a UTop-Prefix query. Although p^* is the largest probability among the probabilities of all the possible k-prefixes, the value of p^* may not be much bigger than the probabilities

τ_i	τ_j	
t_5	t_2	$F(\tau_i, \tau_j) = 6$
t_1	t_5	$K(\tau_i, \tau_j) = 3$
t_2	t_1	$\Delta(\tau^2_i, \tau^2_j) = 2$
t_3	t_4	$I(\tau^2_i, \tau^2_j) = 2$
t_4	t_3	$F^{(3)}(\tau^2_i, \tau^2_j) = 4$
t_6	t_6	

Figure 3.2: Computing the distance between two (partial) lists

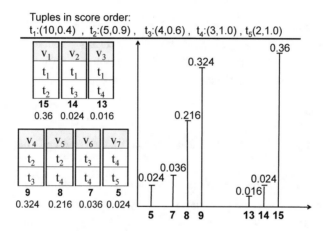

Figure 3.3: Distribution of score summation of top-2 prefixes

of other k-prefixes. Moreover, when the distribution of tuple scores is independent from the distribution of tuple probabilities, UTop-Prefix query answer may be non-typical (i.e., the tuple scores in the UTop-Prefix query answer considerably deviate from the expected score in the distribution of possible k-prefixes).

The previous observations motivated the formulation given by Ge et al. [2009] to define probabilistic ranking query as a task of finding the typical top-k vectors under the tuple uncertainty model. Formally, a set of score values is denoted as the typical top-k scores, according to the following definition:

Definition 3.8 [c-**Typical Top-k Scores**] [**Ge et al., 2009**] Let $\mathcal{S}$ be the probability distribution of the score summation in a k-prefix. Let z be a score value that is randomly chosen from $\mathcal{S}$, and X

be a set of c score values drawn from $\mathcal{S}$. A set of c score values $\{s_1, s_2, \ldots, s_c\}$ is the c-typical top-k scores if $\{s_1, s_2, \ldots, s_c\} = arg \min_X E[\min_{s_i \in X} |z - s_i|]$.   □

For example, consider Figure 3.3, which shows the distribution of score summation in possible 2-prefixes of a set of independent tuples with the shown (score, probability) pairs. The set of 2-typical top-k scores is $\{9, 15\}$ since it minimizes the expected distance to other possible score summation values. We next define probabilistic top-k query based on typical score values:

Definition 3.9   [Uncertain Typical Prefixes Query (UTypical-Prefix)] [Ge et al., 2009] Let $\{s_1, s_2, \ldots, s_c\}$ be the set of c-typical top-k scores. Given a k-prefix v, let $s(v)$ be the summation of score values of the tuples in v. A set of c k-prefixes $\{v_1, \ldots, v_c\}$ is called the c-typical k-prefixes if $v_i = arg \max_{s(v_i)=s_i} \Pr(v_i)$.   □

For example, in Figure 3.3, since the set of 2-typical top-k scores is $\{9, 15\}$, the corresponding set of 2-typical k-prefixes is $\{v_4, v_1\}$, which includes the prefixes achieving the typical score values at the maximum probability. Note that in this example, the set of 2-typical k-prefixes is the same as the two most probable prefixes (i.e., the answer of 2-UTop-Prefix(k) query).

3.3   APPLICATIONS

Proposed semantics of probabilistic ranking queries can be adopted in the following application scenarios:

- A UTop-Prefix query can be used in market analysis to find the most probable product ranking based on evaluations extracted from users' reviews, which may contain uncertain information. Similarly, a UTop-Set query can be used to find a set of products that are most likely to be ranked above all other products.

- A UTop-Rank(i, j) query can be used to find the most probable athlete to end up in a range of ranks in some competition, given a partial order over competitors' strength. A UTop-Rank($1, k$) query can be used to find the most likely location to be in the top-k hottest locations based on uncertain sensor readings represented as intervals.

- The semantics of rank aggregation are widely adopted in many applications related to combining votes from different voters to rank a given set of candidates in a way that minimizes the disagreements of voter's opinions. A typical application is building a meta-search engine (a search engine that aggregates the rankings of multiple other engines) as discussed by Dwork et al. [2001]. An example application of URank-Agg query is preference management in social networking sites where different users rate objects of interest (e.g., photos, videos, products, etc.), inducing a range of possible scores per object. The ratings can be compactly encoded as a PPO. In these settings, finding a consensus ranking can be important for computing recommendations and planning ad campaigns.

CHAPTER 4

Methodologies

In this chapter, we discuss the different methodologies adopted by current proposals to evaluate probabilistic ranking queries. We start our discussion with the methods that build on branch-and-bound search in Section 4.1. We then discuss Monte-Carlo simulation methods in Section 4.2. We give the details of a number of dynamic programming techniques in Section 4.3. We finally describe other methods that build on special properties of probabilistic ranking queries in Section 4.4.

4.1 BRANCH AND BOUND SEARCH

Branch-and-Bound search techniques [Soliman et al., 2010a, 2007, 2008] compute *mode-based* probabilistic ranking queries under both tuple and attribute uncertainty models. The main idea behind this approach is to model top-k query evaluation as a search problem over the space of all possible top-k query answers. In order to navigate such space efficiently, tuples are retrieved in score order to construct the space incrementally.

Query evaluation adopts $\mathcal{A}^*$-like search mechanisms [Hart et al., 1968] to compute query answers from partial space materialization by correctly bounding the probability of different search paths in the space. The search terminates when finding an answer whose probability is not below the probability upper-bound of all unexplored search paths. The proposed techniques have also been shown to minimize the number of consumed tuples and the size of the materialized search space.

We illustrate the branch-and-bound technique in the context of answering UTop-Prefix queries under tuple level uncertainty (Section 4.1.1) and attribute level uncertainty (Section 4.1.2).

4.1.1 UTOP-PREFIX UNDER TUPLE UNCERTAINTY

The basic building block of the search space is the search state, defined as follows:

Definition 4.1 [**Top-l State**] A top-l state s_l is a *prefix* of *length* l of some possible world(s) ordered on a scoring function $\mathcal{F}$. □

A top-l state s_l is *complete* if and only if $l = k$. Based on possible worlds semantics, the probability of state s_l is equal to the summation of the probabilities of all worlds having s_l as a prefix, i.e., a top-l answer. The search for query answers starts from an empty state (with *length* 0) and ends at a goal *complete* state with the maximum probability.

State Probability. Under tuple uncertainty model, we use the notation $\neg X$, where X is a tuple set/vector, to refer to the conjunction of the negation of tuple events in X. Let $\underline{\mathcal{F}}(s_l)$ be the minimum tuple score in s_l. Let I_{s_l} be the set of tuples not in s_l but have higher scores than $\underline{\mathcal{F}}(s_l)$, i.e., $I_{s_l} = \{t | t \in \mathcal{D}, t \notin s_l, \mathcal{F}(t) > \underline{\mathcal{F}}(s_l)\}$. The probability of state s_l, denoted $\mathcal{P}(s_l)$, is equal to the joint probability of the existence of s_l tuples and the absence of I_{s_l} tuples, i.e., $\mathcal{P}(s_l) = \Pr(s_l \wedge \neg I_{s_l})$, which gives the probability that s_l tuples are the top-l vector in the possible worlds space. For example, in Figure 2.1, for a state $s_2 = \langle t1, t5 \rangle$, we have $\mathcal{P}(s_2) = \Pr((t1 \wedge t5) \wedge (\neg t2)) = 0.072$. This result can be verified from ω_4. State probability is computed by taking the dependencies among tuple events into account. The details of probability computations are abstracted by a *Rule Engine* component in the architecture given by Soliman et al. [2007], and we do not discuss here. We next explain an important property of search states.

Property 4.2   [Probability Reduction] When extending any combination of tuple events by adding another tuple existence/absence event, the resulting combination will have at most the same probability. □

Property 4.2 follows from set theory, where a set cannot be larger than its intersection with another set. This holds in the tuple uncertainty model, since for any two sets of tuple events E_n and E_{n+1} (with lengths n and $n + 1$, respectively), where $E_n \subset E_{n+1}$, the set of possible worlds where E_{n+1} is satisfied $\subseteq$ the set of possible worlds where E_n is satisfied.

Soliman et al. [2008] have shown that retrieving tuples in sorted score order is both *necessary* and *sufficient* to get non-trivial bounds on the probabilities of possible complete states. Such bounding is crucial for early query termination, i.e., termination without checking every possible query answer. Sorted score order is also widely adopted by other probabilistic ranking techniques, as we discuss later.

Generating the Search Space. Assume a current state s_l. After retrieving a new tuple t in score order, we extend s_l into two states: (1) $\acute{s}_l$: a state with the same tuple vector as s_l, where we define $I_{\acute{s}_l} = I_{s_l} \cup \{t\}$; and (2) s_{l+1}: a state composed of the tuple vector of s_l appended by t, where $I_{s_{l+1}} = I_{s_l}$. For example, assume a state $s_2 = \langle t1, t2 \rangle$, where $I_{s_2} = \{t3\}$. Hence, $\mathcal{P}(s_2) = \Pr((t1 \wedge t2) \wedge (\neg t3))$. Upon retrieving $t4$, the next tuple in score order, we extend s_2 into (1) $\acute{s}_2 = \langle t1, t2 \rangle$, where $I_{\acute{s}_2} = \{t3, t4\}$, and hence $\mathcal{P}(\acute{s}_2) = \Pr((t1 \wedge t2) \wedge (\neg t3 \wedge \neg t4))$; and (2) $s_3 = \langle t1, t2, t4 \rangle$, where $I_{s_3} = \{t3\}$, and hence $\mathcal{P}(s_3) = \Pr((t1.e \wedge t2 \wedge t4) \wedge (\neg t3))$. Based on Property 4.2, both $\mathcal{P}(\acute{s}_l)$ and $\mathcal{P}(s_{l+1})$ cannot exceed $\mathcal{P}(s_l)$. In addition, $\mathcal{P}(\acute{s}_l) + \mathcal{P}(s_{l+1}) = \mathcal{P}(s_l)$.

The Search Algorithm. We describe Algorithm OPTU-Top$k$ [Soliman et al., 2007] to compute UTop-Prefix(k) query. The details of OPTU-Top$k$ are given in Algorithm 1. The general idea is to buffer retrieved score-ordered tuples and adopt a *lazy* space materialization scheme to extend the state space, i.e., a state might not be extended by all retrieved tuples. At each step, the algorithm extends only the state with the highest probability. State extension is performed using the next tuple

---

Algorithm 1 OptU-Top$k$ Algorithm [Soliman et al., 2007, 2008]

UTop-Prefix (*source* : Score-ordered tuple stream, k : result size)

1    $\mathcal{Q} \leftarrow$ empty p-queue of states ordered on probabilities
2    $d \leftarrow 0$
3    $max_p \leftarrow 0$
4   Insert $s_{0,0}$ into $\mathcal{Q}$ *{initialize $\mathcal{Q}$ with an empty state}*
5   **while** ($\mathcal{Q}$ is not empty)
6   **do**
7            $s_{l,i} \leftarrow$ dequeue $(\mathcal{Q})$ *{get the state with the highest probability}*
8   **if** ($l = k$)
9   **then return** $s_{l,i}$ *{highest probability state is complete, then terminate}*
10   **else**
11                   $t \leftarrow$ NULL
12   **if** ($i = d$)
13   **then** *{need to retrieve a new tuple}*
14   **if** (*source* is not exhausted)
15   **then**
16                                   $t \leftarrow$ get next tuple from *source*
17                                   $d \leftarrow d + 1$
18   **else** *{can use an already retrieved tuple}*
19                               $t \leftarrow$ tuple at pos $i + 1$ in seen tuples buffer
20   **if** (t is not NULL)
21   **then** *{extend states and prune loser ones}*
22   Extend $s_{l,i}$ using t into $s_{l,i+1}, s_{l+1,i+1}$
23   **if** ($l + 1 = k$ AND $\mathcal{P}(s_{l+1,i+1}) > max_p$) **then** $max_p \leftarrow \mathcal{P}(s_{l+1,i+1})$
24   **if** ($\mathcal{P}(s_{l+1,i+1}) \geq max_p$) **then** Insert $s_{l+1,i+1}$ into $\mathcal{Q}$
25   **if** ($\mathcal{P}(s_{l,i+1}) > max_p$) **then** Insert $s_{l,i+1}$ into $\mathcal{Q}$

---

drawn either from the buffer or from the underlying score-ordered tuple retrieval. The algorithm terminates when it reaches a complete state with the highest probability among all possible states.

We now discuss the details of Algorithm 1. We overload state definition s_l to be $s_{l,i}$, where i is the position of the last seen tuple by $s_{l,i}$ in the score-ordered tuple stream. Note that i can point to a buffered tuple or to the next tuple to be retrieved from the *Tuple Access Layer*. We define $s_{0,0}$ as an initial *empty state* of *length* 0, where $\mathcal{P}(s_{0,0}) = 1$. The probability of the empty state upper-bounds the probability of any non-materialized state since any non-materialized state is an extension of the empty state (cf. Property 4.2).

Let $\mathcal{Q}$ be a priority queue of states based on probability where ties are broken using deterministic tie-breaking rules. We initialize $\mathcal{Q}$ with $s_{0,0}$. Let d be the number of retrieved tuples. OPTU-Top$k$ iteratively retrieves the top state in $\mathcal{Q}$, say $s_{l,i}$, extends it into the two next possible states, and inserts the resulting two states back to $\mathcal{Q}$ according to their probabilities. Extending $s_{l,i}$ leads to consuming a new tuple from the *Tuple Access Layer* only if $i = d$; otherwise, $s_{l,i}$ is extended, using the buffered tuple pointed to by $i + 1$.

OPTU-Top$k$ terminates when the top state in Q is a *complete* state. If a *complete* state $s_{k,n}$ is on top of Q, then both materialized and non-materialized states (which are upper-bounded by the empty state) have smaller probabilities than $s_{k,n}$. This means that there is no way to generate another *complete* state that will beat $s_{k,n}$, based on Property 4.2.

In addition to extending the space *lazily*, i.e., only the top Q state is extended at each step, Algorithm 1 also applies a *pruning criterion* to significantly cut down the size of Q (line 20): The algorithm maintains a variable max_p representing the maximum probability of a complete state reached so far. Any other reached state with probability smaller than max_p can be safely pruned (i.e., not inserted in Q), based on Property 4.2.

4.1.2 UTOP-PREFIX UNDER ATTRIBUTE UNCERTAINTY

The previous branch-and-bound algorithm has been extended by Soliman et al. [2010a] to compute UTop-Prefix query under attribute uncertainty. Based on the model in Section 2.2, the rank intervals of different tuples can be derived from the score dominance relationships in the underlying PPO. Using the rank intervals of different tuples, we can incrementally generate candidate top-k prefixes by selecting a distinct tuple, $t_{(i)}$, for each rank, $i = 1 \ldots k$, such that the rank interval of $t_{(i)}$ encloses i, and the selected tuples at different ranks form together a valid top-k prefix (i.e., a prefix of at least one linear extension of the underlying PPO). A top-k prefix v is valid if for each tuple $t_{(i)} \in v$, all tuples dominating $t_{(i)}$ appear in v at ranks smaller than i. For example, in Figure 2.7, the set of tuples that appear at ranks 1 and 2 are $\{t_5, t_2\}$ and $\{t_1, t_2, t_5\}$, respectively. The top-2 prefix $\langle t_2, t_1 \rangle$ is invalid since the tuple t_5, which dominates t_1, is not selected at rank 1. On the other hand, the top-2 prefix $\langle t_5, t_1 \rangle$ is valid since t_1 can be ranked after t_5.

The Search Algorithm.   We use subscripts to denote prefixes' lengths (e.g., v_x is a top-x prefix). Given a top-k prefix v_k, any top-x prefix v_x with $x \leq k$ and $\Pr(v_x) < \Pr(v_k)$ can be safely pruned from the candidates set since $\Pr(v_x)$ upper-bounds the probability of any top-k prefix $\acute{v}_k$ where $v_x \subseteq \acute{v}_k$.

The details of the branch-and-bound search algorithm are given in Algorithm 2. The algorithm works in the following two phases:

- An *initialization phase* that builds and populates the data structures necessary for conducting the search.

- A *searching phase* that applies greedy search heuristics to lazily explore the answer space and prune all candidates that do not lead to query answers.

In the initialization phase, the algorithm reduces the size of the input database, based on the parameter k, by invoking a shrinking algorithm [Soliman and Ilyas, 2009] to remove all tuples whose scores are dominated by the scores of at least k other tuples. The techniques we describe in Section 4.2 are then used to compute $\lambda_{(i,i)}$, the distribution of tuples appearing at each rank $i = 1 \ldots k$. The algorithm maintains k lists $L_1 \ldots L_k$ such that list L_i sorts tuples in $\lambda_{(i,i)}$ in a descending probability order.

Algorithm 2 Branch-and-Bound UTop-Prefix Query Evaluation [Soliman et al., 2010a]

BB-UTop-Prefix $(D : database, k : answer size)$

1   *{Initialization Phase}*
2   $U \leftarrow$ score upper-bound list
3   $\acute{\mathcal{D}} \leftarrow$ Shrink_DB(D, k, U) *{cf. prune k-dominated tuples [Soliman and Ilyas, 2009]}*
4   **for** $i = 1$ **to** k
5   **do**
6   Compute $\lambda_{(i,i)}$ based on $\acute{\mathcal{D}}$ *{cf. Section 4.2}*
7           $L_i \leftarrow$ sort tuples in $\lambda_{(i,i)}$ in a descending prob. order
8   *{Searching Phase}*
9   $\mathcal{Q} \leftarrow$ a priority queue of prefixes ordered on probability
10 $v_0 \leftarrow$ an empty prefix with probability 1
11 $v_0.ptr \leftarrow 0$ *{first position in L_1}*
12 Insert v_0 into $\mathcal{Q}$
13 **while** ($\mathcal{Q}$ is not empty)
14   **do**
15          $v_x^* \leftarrow$ evict top prefix in $\mathcal{Q}$
16   **if** $(x = k)$
17   **then** *{reached query answer}*
18   **return** v_x^*
19          $t^* \leftarrow$ first tuple in L_{x+1} at position $pos^* \geq v_x^*.ptr$
                s.t. $\langle v_x^*, t^* \rangle$ is a valid prefix
20          $v_x^*.ptr \leftarrow pos^* + 1$
21          $v_{x+1} \leftarrow \langle v_x^*, t^* \rangle$
22   Compute $\Pr(v_{x+1})$
23   **if** $(x + 1 = k)$
24   **then**
25   Prune all prefixes in $\mathcal{Q}$ with prob. $< \Pr(v_{x+1})$
26   **else**
27                  $v_{x+1}.ptr \leftarrow 0$ *{first position in L_{x+2}}*
28   **if** $(v_x^*.ptr < |L_{x+1}|)$
29   **then** *{v_x^* can be further extended}*
30                  $\Pr(v_x^*) \leftarrow \Pr(v_x^*) - \Pr(v_{x+1})$
31   Insert v_x^* into $\mathcal{Q}$
32   Insert v_{x+1} into $\mathcal{Q}$

In the searching phase, the algorithm maintains a priority queue $\mathcal{Q}$ that maintains generated candidates in descending order of probability. The priority queue is initialized with an empty prefix v_0 of length 0 and probability 1. Each maintained candidate v_x of length $x < k$ keeps a pointer $v_x.ptr$, pointing at the position of the next tuple in the list L_{x+1} to be used in extending v_x into a candidate of length $x + 1$. Initially, $v_x.ptr$ is set to the first position in L_{x+1}. The positions are assumed to be 0-based. Hence, the value of $v_x.ptr$ ranges between 0 and $|L_{x+1}| - 1$.

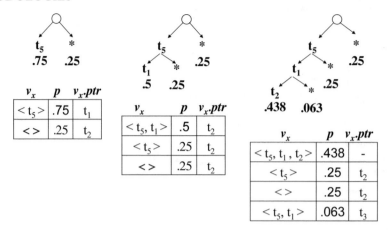

Figure 4.1: Evaluating UTop-Prefix(3) query

Extending candidates is done lazily (i.e., one candidate is extended at a time). Following the greedy criteria of A^* search, the algorithm selects the next candidate to extend as follows. At each iteration, the algorithm evicts the candidate v_x^* at the top of Q (i.e., $\Pr(v_x^*)$ is the highest probability in Q). If $x = k$, the algorithm reports v_x^* as the query answer. Otherwise, if $x < k$, a new candidate v_{x+1} is generated by augmenting v_x^* with the tuple t^* at the first position $\geq v_x^*.ptr$ in L_{x+1} such that $v_{x+1} = \langle v_x^*, t^* \rangle$ is a valid prefix. The pointer $v_x^*.ptr$ is set to the position right after the position of t^* in L_{x+1}, while the pointer $v_{x+1}.ptr$ is set to the first position in L_{x+2} (only if $x + 1 < k$). The probabilities of v_{x+1} and v_x^* are computed ($\Pr(v_x^*)$ is reduced to $\Pr(v_x^*) - \Pr(v_{x+1})$), and the two candidates are reinserted in Q. Furthermore, if $x + 1 = k$ (line 23), the algorithm prunes all candidates in Q whose probabilities are less than $\Pr(v_{x+1})$, according to Property 4.2. Further, if $v_x^*.ptr > |L_{x+1}|$, then v_x^* cannot be extended into candidates of larger length, and so v_x^* is removed from Q.

Figure 4.1 gives an example illustrating how Algorithm 2 works. We use the PPO in Figure 2.7 in this example. Figure 4.1 shows how the branch-and-bound algorithm computes for the answer of a UTop-Prefix(3) query, where the ordered tuples lists $L_1 = \langle t_5, t_2 \rangle$, $L_2 = \langle t_1, t_2, t_5 \rangle$, and $L_3 = \langle t_1, t_2, t_3 \rangle$. The search starts with an empty prefix v_0 with probability 1. The prefix v_0 is extended using t_5 (the first tuple in L_1). The algorithm then computes $\Pr(\langle t_5 \rangle)$ as .75 (the probability is computed using Monte-Carlo integration as discussed in Section 2.2.2), while $\Pr(v_0)$ decreases by .75. Both prefixes are inserted into Q after updating their ptr fields to point to the next tuple that can be used to create valid prefixes later. After three steps, the search terminates since the top prefix in Q has length 3.

4.2   MONTE-CARLO SIMULATION

The basic idea behind Monte-Carlo simulation is to draw samples from a complex probability distribution, representing possible query answers in order to find approximate answers with accuracy proportional to the number of drawn samples. We discuss Monte-Carlo simulation techniques [Soliman and Ilyas, 2009, Soliman et al., 2010a] to compute ranking queries with uncertain scores. Under attribute uncertainty model, given a database D and a parameter k, we denote with $\acute{D}$ the database resulting from pruning tuples in D whose scores are dominated by at least k tuples. Let $\acute{D} = \{t_1, t_2, \ldots, t_n\}$, where $n = |\acute{D}|$. Let Γ be the n-dimensional hypercube that consists of all possible combinations of tuples' scores. That is, $\Gamma = ([lo_1, up_1] \times [lo_2, up_2] \times \cdots \times [lo_n, up_n])$. A vector $\gamma = (x_1, x_2, \ldots, x_n)$ of n real values, where $x_i \in [lo_i, up_i]$, represents one point in Γ. Let $\Pi_{\acute{D}}(\gamma) = \prod_{i=1}^{n} f_i(x_i)$, where f_i is the score density of tuple t_i. Tuples with deterministic (single-valued) scores are represented by the same score value in all possible γ's. On the other hand, tuples with uncertain scores can be represented by different score values in different γ's, according to the intervals that enclose their possible scores.

In case of a continuous f_i, the component x_i is assumed to be a tiny score interval in $[lo_i, up_i]$, and $f_i(x_i)$ is the result of integrating f_i over x_i. We assume that the components x_i's of any possible vector $\gamma = (x_1, x_2, \ldots, x_n)$ can always be totally ordered based on their values.

4.2.1   COMPUTING UTOP-RANK QUERY

The main insight behind computing UTop-Rank(i, j) query is transforming the complex space of linear extensions, which have to be aggregated to compute query answer, to the simpler space of all possible score combinations Γ. Such space can be sampled uniformly and independently to find the probability of query answer without enumerating the linear extensions. The accuracy of the result depends only on the number of drawn samples s (Monte-Carlo method guarantees that the approximation error is in $O(\frac{1}{\sqrt{s}})$).

For a tuple t_k, we draw a sample $\gamma \in \Gamma$ as follows:

1. Generate the value x_k in γ.

2. Generate $n - 1$ independent values for other components in γ one by one.

3. If at any point there are j values in γ greater than x_k, reject γ.

4. Eventually, if the rank of x_k in γ is in $i \ldots j$, accept γ.

Let $\lambda_{(i,j)}(t_k)$ be the probability of t_k to appear at rank $i \ldots j$. The above procedure describes a sampler that can be used to evaluate the following integral using the Monte-Carlo integration method described in Section 2.2.2:

$$\lambda_{(i,j)}(t_k) = \int_{\Gamma_{(i,j,t_k)}} \Pi_{\acute{D}}(\gamma) \, d\gamma \qquad (4.1)$$

where $\Gamma_{(i,j,t_k)} \subseteq \Gamma$ is the volume defined by the points $\gamma = (x_1, \ldots, x_n)$, with x_k's rank is in $i \ldots j$. The integral in Equation 4.1 is evaluated as discussed in Section 2.2.2.

4.2.2   COMPUTING UTOP-PREFIX AND UTOP-SET QUERIES

Let v be an ordered list of k tuples and s be a set of k tuples. We denote with $\Pr(v)$ the top-k prefix probability of v and, similarly, we denote with $\Pr(s)$ the top-k set probability of s.

Similar to the discussion of UTop-Rank queries in Section 4.2.1, $\Pr(v)$ is computed using Monte-Carlo integration on the volume $\Gamma_{(v)} \subseteq \Gamma$, which consists of the points $\gamma = (x_1, \ldots, x_n)$ such that the values in γ that correspond to tuples in v have the same ranking as the ranking of tuples in v, and any other value in γ is smaller than the value corresponding to the last tuple in v. On the other hand, $\Pr(s)$ is computed by integrating on the volume $\Gamma_{(u)} \subseteq \Gamma$, which consists of the points $\gamma = (x_1, \ldots, x_n)$ such that any value in γ, that does not correspond to a tuple in s, is smaller than the minimum value that corresponds to a tuple in s.

The cost of the above integrals is similar to the cost of the integral in Equation 4.1 (mainly proportional to the number of samples). However, the number of integrals we need to evaluate here is exponential (one integral per each top-k prefix/set), while it is linear for UTop-Rank queries (one integral per each tuple). The distribution of top-k prefixes/sets can be simulated using the Metropolis-Hastings (M-H) algorithm [Hastings, 1970] to approximate the most probable query answers. The (M-H) algorithm falls in the class of Markov Chains Monte-Carlo (MCMC) methods, which combine the concepts of Monte-Carlo method and Markov chains to simulate a complex distribution using a Markovian sampling process, where each sample depends only on the previous sample. We discuss the details in the following.

Sampling Space.   A state in the sampling space is a linear extension ω of the PPO induced by $\hat{\mathcal{D}}$. Let θ and Θ be the distributions of the top-k prefix probabilities and top-k set probabilities, respectively. Let $\pi(\omega)$ be the probability of the top-k prefix or the top-k set in ω, depending on whether we simulate θ or Θ, respectively. The objective is to *propose* states with high probabilities in a light-weight fashion. This is done by shuffling the ranking of tuples in ω biased by the weights of pairwise rankings (Equation 2.1). This approach guarantees sampling valid linear extensions since ranks are shuffled only when tuples probabilistically dominate each other.

Given a state ω_i, a candidate state ω_{i+1} is generated as follows:

1. Generate a random number $z \in [1, k]$.

2. For $j = 1 \ldots z$, do the following:

   (a) Randomly pick a rank r_j in ω_i. Let $t_{(r_j)}$ be the tuple at rank r_j in ω_i.

   (b) If $r_j \in [1, k]$, move $t_{(r_j)}$ downward in ω_i; otherwise, move $t_{(r_j)}$ upward. This is done by swapping $t_{(r_j)}$ with lower tuples in ω_i if $r_j \in [1, k]$, or with upper tuples if $r_j \notin [1, k]$. Swaps are conducted one by one, where swapping tuples $t_{(r_j)}$ and $t_{(m)}$

is committed with probability $P_{(r_j,m)} = \Pr(t_{(r_j)} > t_{(m)})$ if $r_j > m$, or with probability $P_{(m,r_j)} = \Pr(t_{(m)} > t_{(r_j)})$, otherwise. Tuple swapping stops at the first uncommitted swap.

The (M-H) algorithm is proven to converge with arbitrary proposal distributions [Hastings, 1970]. The proposal distribution $q(\omega_{i+1}|\omega_i)$ is defined as follows. In the above sample generator, at each step j, assume that $t_{(r_j)}$ has moved to a rank $r < r_j$. Let $R_{(r_j,r)} = \{r_j - 1, r_j - 2, \ldots, r\}$. Let $P_j = \prod_{m \in R_{(r_j,r)}} P_{(r_j,m)}$. Similarly, P_j can be defined for $r > r_j$. Then, the proposal distribution $q(\omega_{i+1}|\omega_i) = \prod_{j=1}^{z} P_j$, due to independence of steps. Based on the (M-H) algorithm, ω_{i+1} is accepted with probability $\alpha = min(\frac{\pi(\omega_{i+1}).q(\omega_i|\omega_{i+1})}{\pi(\omega_i).q(\omega_{i+1}|\omega_i)}, 1)$.

Computing Query Answers. The (M-H) sampler simulates the top-k prefixes/sets distribution using a Markov chain (a random walk) that visits states biased by probability. Gelman and Rubin [1992] have argued that it is not generally possible to use a single simulation to infer distribution characteristics. The main problem is that the initial state may trap the random walk for many iterations in some region in the target distribution. The problem is solved by taking dispersed starting states and running multiple iterative simulations that independently explore the underlying distribution.

We thus run multiple independent Markov chains, where each chain starts from an independently selected initial state, and each chain simulates the space independently of all other chains. The initial state of each chain is obtained by independently selecting a random score value from each score interval and ranking the tuples based on the drawn scores, resulting in a valid linear extension.

A crucial point is determining whether the chains have mixed with the target distribution (i.e., whether the current status of the simulation closely approximates the target distribution). At mixing time, which is determined based on Gelman-Rubin diagnostic [Gelman and Rubin, 1992], the Markov chains produce samples that closely follow the target distribution and hence can be used to infer distribution characteristics.

At mixing time, which is determined by the value of convergence diagnostic, each chain approximates the distribution's mode as the most probable visited state (similar to simulated annealing). The l most probable visited states across all chains approximate the l-UTop-Prefix (or l-UTop-Set) query answers.

4.3   DYNAMIC PROGRAMMING

A number of different proposals employ dynamic programming techniques to compute probabilistic ranking queries with different semantics. A dynamic programming solution applies to problems with the *optimal substructure* property (i.e., the optimal solution of the larger problem is constructed from optimal solutions of smaller problems). As we show in the next sections, multiple formulations of the probabilistic ranking problems have been shown to satisfy the optimal substructure property, allowing for designing efficient dynamic programming solutions.

| Score-ranked stream | t1:0.3 | t2:0.9 | t3:0.6 | t4:0.25 | t5:0.8 | ... |

	t1	t2	t3	t4	t5
Rank 1	0.3	0.63	0.042	0.007	0.0168
Rank 2	0	0.27	0.396	0.0765	0.1892
Rank 3	0	0	0.162	0.126	0.3636

Figure 4.2: IndepU-kRanks processing steps

4.3.1   UTOP-RANK QUERY UNDER INDEPENDENCE

The first dynamic programming algorithm to solve a probabilistic ranking problem is IndepU-kRanks [Soliman et al., 2007], which addresses computing UTop-Rank(i, i) query under the tuple uncertainty model with independent tuple events.

Consider the example depicted by Figure 4.2, where we are interested in UTop-Rank(i, i) query answer, for $i = 1$ to 3. In the shown table, a cell at row i and column x contains $\Pr(x, i)$ (the probability of tuple x to be at rank i). For a scoring function $\mathcal{F}$, the rank 1 probability of a tuple x is computed as $\Pr(x) \times \prod_{z:\mathcal{F}(x)<\mathcal{F}(z)} (1 - \Pr(z))$, which is the probability that the event of tuple x is true and all tuple events with higher scores are false. The computation of the probabilities in the remaining rows is based on the following property:

Property 4.3   **[Recurrence of Rank Probability]** Under tuple independence and for $i > 1$,

$$\Pr(x, i) = \Pr(x) \times \sum_{y:\mathcal{F}(y)>\mathcal{F}(x)} \Pr(y, i - 1) \times \prod_{z:\mathcal{F}(x)<\mathcal{F}(z)<\mathcal{F}(y)} (1 - \Pr(z))$$

$\square$

The rationale of Property 4.3 is that under independence for tuple x to appear at rank i, we need only to consider the probability that x is consecutive to every other tuple y at rank $i - 1$. This probability is computed using the probability that x exists, each tuple z that appears at an intermediate rank between x and y does not exist, and y appears at rank $i - 1$.

For example, in Figure 4.2, $\Pr(t2, 2) = 0.9 \times 0.3 = 0.27$, while $\Pr(t3, 2) = (0.6 \times 0.63) + (0.6 \times 0.1 \times 0.3) = 0.396$. The shaded cells indicate the UTop-Rank(i, i) answer, for $i = 1$ to 3. Notice that the summation of the probabilities of each row will be 1 if we completely exhaust the tuple stream. This is because each row actually represents a horizontal *slice* in ranked possible worlds. This means that we can report an answer from any row whenever the maximum probability in that row is greater than the row probability remainder. Notice also that the computation in each row depends solely on the row above.

The above description gives rise to the following dynamic programming formulation. We construct a matrix M with k rows (where k is the number of required top ranks in the top-k query), and a new column is added to M whenever we retrieve a new tuple from the score-ranked stream. Upon retrieving a new tuple t, the column of t in M is filled downwards based on the following equation:

$$
M[i, t] = \begin{cases}
\Pr(t) \times \displaystyle\prod_{z:\mathcal{F}(t)<\mathcal{F}(z)} (1 - \Pr(z)) & \text{if } i = 1 \\[2em]
\Pr(t) \times \displaystyle\sum_{y:\mathcal{F}(y)>\mathcal{F}(t)} M[i-1, y] \times \prod_{z:\mathcal{F}(t)<\mathcal{F}(z)<\mathcal{F}(y)} (1 - \Pr(z)) & \text{if } i > 1
\end{cases}
\tag{4.2}
$$

For example, in Figure 4.2, $M[2, 3] = \Pr(t3) \times (M[1, 2] + (1 - \Pr(t2)) \times M[1, 1])$. The algorithm returns a set of k tuples $\{t_1 \ldots t_k\}$, where $t_i = argmax_x \, M[i, x]$.

Since the size of the matrix M is in $O(nk)$, where n is the number of consumed tuples in score order, and for each consumed tuple, the algorithm scans the matrix rows to compute tuple probability at each rank, the total time complexity is thus $O(n^2 k)$.

4.3.2   GENERATING FUNCTIONS

Li and Deshpande [2009] have shown that the probability of a tuple to appear at each rank can be given by the coefficients of a recursively constructed polynomial. Assume a tuple uncertainty model, where all tuple events are independent. Assume that tuples based on score order are given as $\langle t_1, t_2, \ldots, t_n \rangle$. Recall that $\Pr(t, i)$ is the probability of tuple t to appear at rank i in a random possible world.

To understand the polynomial construction, consider 2 tuples $\langle t_1, t_2 \rangle$. Then, we have $\Pr(t_2, 1) = (1 - \Pr(t_1)) \cdot \Pr(t_2)$, and $\Pr(t_2, 2) = \Pr(t_1) \cdot \Pr(t_2)$. When there are 3 tuples $\langle t_1, t_2, t_3 \rangle$, we have $\Pr(t_3, 1) = (1 - \Pr(t_1)) \cdot (1 - \Pr(t_2)) \cdot \Pr(t_3)$, $\Pr(t_3, 2) = ((1 - \Pr(t_1)) \cdot \Pr(t_2) + (1 - \Pr(t_2)) \cdot \Pr(t_1)) \cdot \Pr(t_3)$, and $\Pr(t_3, 3) = \Pr(t_1) \cdot \Pr(t_2) \cdot \Pr(t_3)$. In general, consider the polynomial $\mathcal{F}^i(x)$, defined as follows:

$$
\mathcal{F}^i(x) = \Big(\prod_{j<i}(1 - \Pr(t_j) + \Pr(t_j) \cdot x)\Big) \cdot (\Pr(t_i) \cdot x) = \sum_{j \geq 1} c_j x^j
\tag{4.3}
$$

The coefficient of x^j in the polynomial $\mathcal{F}^i(x)$ is the same as $\Pr(t_i, j)$. For a given tuple t_i, a simple algorithm to compute $\Pr(t_i, j)$ for all possible j values has the complexity $O(i^2)$, which is the cost of expanding $\mathcal{F}^i(x)$. The total complexity of computing $\mathcal{F}^i(x)$ over all tuples is thus $O(n^3)$. However, Li et al. [2009] have shown that the expansion of the polynomial $\mathcal{F}^i(x)$ can be done more efficiently in $O(i)$, using the expansion of the polynomial $\mathcal{F}^{i-1}(x)$, based on the following dynamic programming formulation:

$$
\mathcal{F}^i(x) = \frac{\Pr(t_i)}{\Pr(t_{i-1})} \, \mathcal{F}^{i-1}(x) \, (1 - \Pr(t_{i-1}) + \Pr(t_{i-1}) \cdot x)
\tag{4.4}
$$

Algorithm 3 IND-PRF-RANK [Li et al., 2009]

---

1   $\mathcal{F}^0(x) = 1$

2   **for** $(i = 1$ to $n)$

3   **do**

4            $\mathcal{F}^i(x) = \frac{\Pr(t_i)}{\Pr(t_{i-1})} \mathcal{F}^{i-1}(x)\,(1 - \Pr(t_{i-1}) + \Pr(t_{i-1}) \cdot x)$

5   Expand $\mathcal{F}^i(x)$ as $\sum_{j \geq 1} c_j x^j$

Hence, the total complexity of computing $\Pr(t_i, j)$ for all possible i and j values is $O(n^2)$. Algorithm 3 gives the pseudo code of this technique.

Extending the previous dynamic programming formulation to handle discrete attribute uncertainty model is done using the And/Xor tree model discussed in Section 2.2.1. Assume that we would like to compute the distribution of possible ranks of a tuple instance t. For each tree node u, we compute the polynomial $\mathcal{F}_u$, recursively, as follows:

- If u is a leaf node, $\mathcal{F}_u = \begin{cases} y & \textit{if } u = t \\ x & \textit{if } score(u) > score(t) \\ 1 & \textit{otherwise} \end{cases}$

- If u is a $(\vee)$ node, $\mathcal{F}_u = (1 - \sum_{v \in children(u)} P_{u,v}) + \sum_{v \in children(u)} P_{u,v} \cdot \mathcal{F}_v$.

- If u is a $(\wedge)$ node, $\mathcal{F}_u = \Pi_{v \in children(u)} \mathcal{F}_v$.

Let τ be the root of the and/xor tree. Then, $\Pr(t, i)$ is given by the coefficient of $(x^{i-1}.y)$ in the polynomial $\mathcal{F}_\tau$. For example, in Figure 2.5, the probability of $r4.1$ to appear at rank 1 is 0.072, based on the possible worlds shown in Figure 2.1 ($r4.1$ corresponds to tuple $t6$, which appears at rank 1 only in ω_7). We show, in Figure 4.3, the polynomial corresponding to $r4.1$: $\mathcal{F}_\tau = 0.072y + 0.396xy + 0.712x^2y + 0.42x^3y$. For $i = 1$, the coefficient of $(x^{i-1}.y)$ is 0.072, which is the probability of $r4.1$ to appear at rank 1. Since $r4$ has only one instance, $r4.1$, this probability is the same as the probability of $r4$ to appear at rank 1. If, alternatively, we would like to compute $\Pr(r3, i)$, we need to sum up $\Pr(r3.1, i)$ and $\Pr(r3.2, i)$.

Based on the computed values of $\Pr(t, j)$, Li et al. [2009] have proposed a framework that encapsulates a number of probabilistic ranking query semantics. The framework is based on the notion of *generating functions*. For a tuple t, the generating function $\Upsilon(t)$ is defined as follows:

$$\Upsilon(t) = \sum_{j \geq 1} w(t, j) \cdot \Pr(t, j) \tag{4.5}$$

where $w(t, j)$ is a weight function assigned to the occurrence of tuple t at rank j.

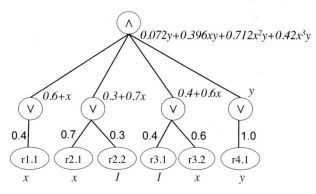

Figure 4.3: Computing the rank distribution of $r4.1$ using And/Xor tree

When tuples are ranked based on the value of $\Upsilon(t)$, we obtain rankings under different semantics of probabilistic ranking queries, depending on how we the set the value of the weight function $w(t, j)$. For example, consider the following settings of $w(t, j)$:

- If $w(t, j) = 1$, the result is the ranking of tuples based on their membership probabilities [Ré et al., 2007].

- If $w(t, j) = score(t)$, the result is the ranking of tuples based on their expected scores.

- If $w(t, j) = \begin{cases} 1 & if\ i_1 \leq j \leq i_2 \\ 0 & otherwise \end{cases}$, then the tuple with the largest $\Upsilon(t)$ value is the same as the UTop-Rank(i_1, i_2) query answer [Soliman and Ilyas, 2009, Soliman et al., 2007]. This also allows representing other semantics such as Global Top-k [Zhang and Chomicki, 2009] and PT-k [Hua et al., 2008], as we show in Section 3.1.

4.3.3 PROBABILISTIC THRESHOLD

We discuss the algorithm given by Hua et al. [2008] to compute Probabilistic Threshold top-k (PT-k) query, defined in Section 3.1. Given a probability threshold T and a parameter k, the objective is to find all tuples whose UTop-Rank$(1, k)$ probabilities are at least T.

Let $\langle t_1, t_2, \ldots, t_n \rangle$ be the set of tuples ordered on score. For a tuple t_i, we denote with S_{t_i} the set of tuples preceding t_i in score order. Under the tuple uncertainty model with independent tuple events, let $\Pr^k(t_i)$ be the probability that t_i is ranked at position $1 \ldots k$ inclusive in a random possible world. A tuple t_i appears at position j in a ranked possible world w if a subset of exactly $j - 1$ tuples in S_{t_i} also appears in w. For a tuple t_i with $i \leq k$, we have $|S_{t_i}| < k$, and hence $\Pr^k(t_i) = \Pr(t_i)$. On the other hand, for a tuple t_i with $i > k$, we have $\Pr^k(t_i) < \Pr(t_i)$.

Let $\Pr(S_{t_i}, j)$ be the probability that exactly j tuples in S_{t_i} appear in a random possible world, where $\Pr(\phi, 0) = 1$ and $\Pr(\phi, j) = 0$ for all $j > 0$. For $S_{t_i} \neq \phi$, a possible world w contributes to

Tuples in score order:
t_1:0.3 , t_2: 0.9 , t_3:0.6 , t_4:0.25 , t_5:0.8

	j = 0	j = 1	j = 2	j = 3
t_1	1.0	0	0	0
t_2	0.7	0.3	0	0
t_3	0.07	0.66	0.27	0
t_4	0.028	(0.07 x 0.6) + (0.66 x 0.4) = 0.306	0.504	0.162
t_5	0.021	0.2365	0.4545	0.2475

Figure 4.4: Computing $\Pr(S_{t_i}, j)$ for independent tuples

$\Pr(S_{t_i}, j)$ in one of two cases: (1) the tuple $t_{i-1} \in w$, which means that $j - 1$ other tuples from S_{t_i} must also appear in w, and (2) the tuple $t_{i-1} \notin w$, which means that j other tuples from S_{t_i} must appear in w. This recursive relation can be expressed as we show in Equation 4.6:

$$\Pr(S_{t_i}, j) = \begin{cases} 1 & if \; i = 1 \wedge j = 0 \\ 0 & if \; i = 1 \wedge j > 0 \\ \prod_{m=1}^{i-1}(1 - \Pr(t_m)) & if \; i > 1 \wedge j = 0 \\ \Pr(S_{t_{i-1}}, j - 1) \cdot \Pr(t_{i-1}) + \Pr(S_{t_{i-1}}, j) \cdot (1 - \Pr(t_{i-1})) & if \; i > 1 \wedge j > 0 \end{cases} \quad (4.6)$$

For example, Figure 4.4 shows how to compute $\Pr(S_{t_i}, j)$ using dynamic programming for the example of independent tuples used in Figure 4.2. Given n tuples and a parameter k, we construct a matrix M of n rows (corresponding to the n tuples in score order) and $k + 1$ columns (corresponding to the values $0 \ldots k$). Based on the recurrence relation in Equation 4.6, the cell $M[t_1, 0] = 1$, while $M[t_1, j] = 0$ for $j > 0$. Each cell $M[t_i, 0] = \prod_{m<i}(1 - \Pr(t_m))$. Finally, each cell $M[t_i, j]$, for $j > 0$ and $i > 1$, is computed using the values of $M[t_{i-1}, j - 1]$ and $M[t_{i-1}, j]$. For example, in Figure 4.4, the value in the shaded cell $M[t_4, 1]$ is given by $M[t_3, 0] \cdot \Pr(t_2) + M[t_3, 1] \cdot (1 - \Pr(t_2))$.

Based on the computed values of $\Pr(S_{t_i}, j)$ for $j < k$, we can compute the value of $\Pr^k(t_i)$ as follows:

$$\Pr^k(t_i) = \sum_{j=1}^{k} \Pr(t_i, j) = \Pr(t_i) \sum_{j=0}^{k-1} \Pr(S_{t_i}, j)$$

The previous algorithm computes $\Pr^k(t_i)$ of n tuples in $O(nk)$. Extending the previous algorithm to handle dependencies in the form of mutual exclusion rules, with every tuple belonging to at most one rule, has been also discussed by Hua et al. [2008].

4.3.4 TYPICAL TOP-k ANSWERS

We describe the algorithm given by Ge et al. [2009] to compute UTypical-Prefix query, defined in Section 3.2. We refer to the k-length prefixes of ranked possible worlds as 'k-prefixes' for short. The

Tuples in score order:
t_1:(10,0.4) , t_2:(5,0.9) , t_3:(4,0.6) , t_4:(3,1.0) , t_5(2,1.0)

	2	1	0
t_1	{(5,0.024),(7,0.036),(8,0.216), (9,0.324),(13,0.016),(14,0.024), (15,0.36)}	{(3,0.024),(4,0.036), (5,0.54),(10,0.4)}	{(0,1.0)}
t_2	{(5,0.04),(7,0.06),(8,0.36), (9,0.54)}	{(3,0.04),(4,0.06), (5,0.9)}	{(0,1.0)}
t_3	{(5,0.4),(7,0.6)}	{(3,0.4),(4,0.6)}	{(0,1.0)}
t_4	{(5,1.0)}	{(3,1.0)}	{(0,1.0)}
t_5	{(0,0)}	{(2,1.0)}	{(0,1.0)}

Figure 4.5: Computing distribution of score summation using dynamic programming

algorithm computes the distribution of score summation of possible k-prefixes, and it returns typical k-prefixes in that distribution.

A straightforward approach to compute the distribution of score summation of k-prefixes is the following: i) materialize the possible worlds, ii) find distinct s values, where s is the summation of scores in a possible k-prefix, and iii) add up the probabilities of every set of worlds yielding the same s value. Except for a very small number of tuples, this approach can be very expensive.

The distribution of score summation can be computed much more efficiently using the dynamic programming algorithm given by Ge et al. [2009]. Consider the table shown in Figure 4.5, which illustrates the computation of the distribution of score summation of the 2-prefixes of the score ordered tuples shown at the top (this is the same example given in Figure 3.3). The table has one row per tuple in the order of tuple scores and one column per each rank starting from k down to 0. The cells of column 0 are all initialized by the distribution {(0, 1.0)}. The cell (t_i, j) contains the distribution of score summation in possible j-prefixes of tuples starting from t_i. For example, the cell $(t_5, 1)$ contains the distribution of possible 1-prefixes of $\langle t_3, t_4, t_5 \rangle$. This distribution has two (score summation, probability) pairs: $(3, 0.4)$, which corresponds to the 1-prefix $\langle \neg t_3, t_4 \rangle$, and $(4, 0.6)$, which corresponds to the 1-prefix $\langle t_3 \rangle$. Based on tuple probabilities and scores, these are the only possible 1-prefixes starting from t_3.

The distributions table is filled upwards, starting from the bottom row with the objective of finding the distribution at the cell (t_1, k) (the shaded cell in Figure 4.5). In general, let $D_{i,j}$ be the distribution at cell (i, j). Under tuple independence, $D_{i,j}$ can be computed efficiently from $D_{i+1,j}$ and $D_{i+1,j-1}$ by the following recurrence relation:

1. For each $(s, p) \in D_{i+1,j}$, add to $D_{i,j}$ the pair $(s, p \cdot (1 - \Pr(t_i)))$.

2. For each $(s, p) \in D_{i+1,j-1}$, add to $D_{i,j}$ the pair $(s + score(t_i), p \cdot \Pr(t_i))$.

3. Merge the pairs with identical s values in $D_{i,j}$ by summing up their probabilities.

The first step adds to $D_{i,j}$ the j-prefixes in $D_{i+1,j}$ by considering t_i absent. The second step adds to $D_{i,j}$ the j-prefixes generated by appending t_i to the $(j-1)$ prefixes included in $D_{i+1,j-1}$. The third step merges identical score values generated in the two previous steps.

The previous algorithm has been also extended by Ge et al. [2009] to handle dependencies among tuples in the form of mutual exclusion rules.

4.4   OTHER METHODOLOGIES

In this section, we discuss techniques that are based on observations and special properties pertinent to different formulations of the probabilistic ranking problem.

4.4.1   EXPECTED RANKS

For the discrete score uncertainty model (cf. Section 2.2.1), Cormode et al. [2009] have shown that computing the expected ranks of a set of n tuples can be done in $O(n log(n))$ under the assumption that the number of possible scores per tuple is bounded by some constant. We describe the main algorithm in the following.

Let $\{t_1, \ldots, t_n\}$ be a set of tuples with discrete uncertain scores. Let X_i be a random variable representing the possible scores of t_i, where the set of possible values of X_i are $\{v_{i,1}, \ldots, v_{i,s_i}\}$ and their corresponding probabilities are $\{p_{i,1}, \ldots, p_{i,s_i}\}$. For every tuple t_i, we assume that $s_i \leq s$, where s is some constant. By linearity of expectation, we can express $ER(t_i)$ as $\sum_{i \neq j} \Pr(X_j > X_i)$, which can be rewritten as follows:

$$
\begin{aligned}
ER(t_i) &= \sum_{i \neq j} \Pr(X_j > X_i) = \sum_{i \neq j} \sum_{l=1}^{s_i} p_{i,l} \cdot \Pr(X_j > v_{i,l}) \\
&= \sum_{l=1}^{s_i} p_{i,l} \cdot \sum_{i \neq j} \Pr(X_j > v_{i,l}) \\
&= \sum_{l=1}^{s_i} p_{i,l} \cdot \left(\sum_j \Pr(X_j > v_{i,l}) - \Pr(X_i > v_{i,l}) \right) \\
&= \sum_{l=1}^{s_i} p_{i,l} \cdot (q(v_{i,l}) - \Pr(X_i > v_{i,l}))
\end{aligned}
$$

where $q(v) = \sum_j \Pr(X_j > v)$.

Let U be the universe of possible scores of all tuples. Based on the assumption that the number of possible scores per tuple is bounded by a constant, the size of U is linear in n. By sorting U, the quantity $q(v)$ can be computed in a linear pass over the sorted values in U. Given the value of

$q(v)$ for each possible value $v \in U$, $ER(t)$ is computed in constant time. It follows that the overall complexity of the algorithm is $O(nlog(n))$.

Cormode et al. [2009] have also extended the previous algorithm to find expected ranks under the tuple uncertainty model (cf. Section 2.1), and they have introduced optimizations when only the k tuples with the highest expected ranks are required.

4.4.2   UNCERTAIN RANK AGGREGATION

Rank aggregation is the problem of computing a consensus ranking for a set of candidates using input rankings of the candidates coming from different voters. The problem has immediate applications in Web meta-search engines [Dwork et al., 2001].

The optimal rank aggregation is the ranking with the minimum average distance to all input rankings. A strong resemblance exists between ranking in possible worlds and the rank aggregation problem. By viewing possible worlds as voters and tuples as candidates, we obtain an instance of the rank aggregation problem. However, rank aggregation on uncertain data has two main distinctions: i) there is a weight (probability) associated with each voter, and ii) the rankings given by the voters can be partial since possible worlds may be subsets of database tuples. A number of proposals [Li and Deshpande, 2009, Soliman and Ilyas, 2009, Soliman et al., 2010a] have investigated evaluation algorithms of rank aggregation queries on uncertain data under two different problem formulations:

- *Optimal rank aggregation on full lists.* This formulation applies to attribute uncertainty models, where ranked possible worlds are full orderings (permutations) of all tuples.

- *Optimal rank aggregation on partial lists.* This formulation applies to tuple uncertainty models, where ranked possible worlds may give partial rankings (i.e., rankings of different subsets of tuples). The same formulation applies to optimal aggregation of top-k lists.

The main difference between the two formulations is the definition of the function that computes the distance between two (partial) rankings.

Computing Rank Aggregation on Full Lists We describe the algorithms proposed by Soliman and Ilyas [2009], Soliman et al. [2010a] to solve the rank aggregation problem under attribute uncertainty model. The described algorithms support two widely used distance functions: footrule distance and Kendall tau distance, defined in Section 3.2.

URank-Agg with Footrule Distance. Optimal rank aggregation under footrule distance can be computed in polynomial time by the following algorithm, proposed by Dwork et al. [2001]. Given a set of rankings $\omega_1 \ldots \omega_m$, the objective is to find the optimal ranking ω^* that minimizes $\frac{1}{m} \sum_{i=1}^{m} F(\omega^*, \omega_i)$. The problem is modeled using a weighted bipartite graph G with two sets of nodes. The first set has a node for each candidate, while the second set has a node for each rank. Each candidate c and rank r are connected with an edge (c, r) whose weight $w(c, r) = \sum_{i=1}^{m} |\omega_i(c) - r|$. Then, ω^* (the optimal ranking) is given by "the minimum cost perfect matching" of G, where a

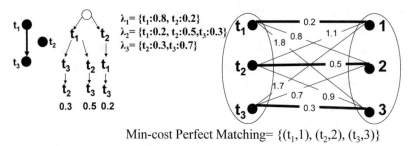

Min-cost Perfect Matching= $\{(t_1,1), (t_2,2), (t_3,3)\}$

Figure 4.6: Bipartite graph matching

perfect matching is a subset of graph edges such that every node is connected to exactly one edge, while the matching cost is the summation of the weights of its edges. Finding such matching can be done in $O(n^{2.5})$, where n is the number of graph nodes [Dwork et al., 2001].

Given a PPO capturing attribute uncertainty (Section 2.2.2), each linear extension is viewed as a voter, and the objective is to find the optimal linear extension that has the minimum average distance to all voters. This problem can be solved in polynomial time, given the probability distribution λ_i (the distribution of different tuples to appear at rank i) for each rank i.

The distributions λ_i's provide compact summaries of voter's opinions, which allows computing the edge weights in the bipartite graph without expanding the space of linear extensions. Specifically, it has been shown that the weight $w(t, r)$ (in the previous bipartite graph model) is proportional to $\sum_{j=1}^{n}(\lambda_j(t) \times |j - r|)$ [Soliman and Ilyas, 2009]. The distributions λ_i's are obtained by applying Equation 4.1 at each rank i separately, yielding a quadratic cost in the number of tuples n.

Figure 4.6 shows an example illustrating this technique. The probabilities of the depicted linear extensions are summarized as λ_i's without expanding the space (Section 4.2.1). The λ_i's are used to compute the weights in the bipartite graph yielding $\langle t_1, t_2, t_3 \rangle$ as the optimal linear extension.

URank-Agg with Kendall Tau Distance. Optimal rank aggregation under Kendall tau distance is known to be NP-Hard, in general, by reduction to the problem of minimum feedback arc set [Kenyon-Mathieu and Schudy, 2007]: Construct a complete weighted directed graph whose nodes are the candidates, such that an edge connecting nodes c_i and c_j is weighted by the proportion of voters who rank c_i before c_j. The problem is to find the set of edges with the minimum weight summation whose removal converts the input graph to a DAG. Since the input graph is complete, the resulting DAG defines a total order on the set of candidates, which is the optimal rank aggregation.

The hardness of the rank aggregation problem gives rise to approximation methods similar to the Markov chains-based methods, given by Dwork et al. [2001] to find the optimal rank aggregation. Spearman footrule aggregation is also known to be a 2-approximation of Kendall tau aggregation [Kenyon-Mathieu and Schudy, 2007].

Soliman et al. [2010a] have shown that the property of weak stochastic transitivity can be used to identify classes of PPO's in which computing optimal rank aggregation has only polynomial time cost.

Definition 4.4   [Weak Stochastic Transitivity] [van Acker, 1990] A PPO is weak stochastic transitive iff $\forall$ tuples $x, y, z : [\Pr(x > y) \geq 0.5$ and $\Pr(y > z) \geq 0.5] \Rightarrow \Pr(x > z) \geq 0.5$.   □

Given an input PPO, the property of weak stochastic transitivity can be decided in $O(n^3)$, where n is the database size, since the property needs to be checked on tuple triples. Let $\omega(t)$ denote the position of tuple t in the ranking ω. For a weak stochastic transitive PPO, Soliman et al. [2010a] have shown that the optimal rank aggregation ω^* under Kendall tau distance is given by the following rule:

$$\forall \ tuples \ x, y : [\omega^*(x) < \omega^*(y)] \Leftrightarrow [\Pr(x > y) \geq 0.5]$$

The previous result allows for an efficient evaluation procedure, where $\Pr(x > y)$ is computed for each pair of tuples (x, y), and then the computed probabilities are used to sort the tuples. That is, starting from an arbitrary ranking of tuples, the positions of two tuples x and y need to be swapped iff $\Pr(x > y) \geq 0.5$ and x is ranked below y. Based on the weak stochastic transitivity of the PPO, this procedure yields a valid ranking of tuples since transitivity does not introduce cycles in the relative order of tuples. Hence, the overall complexity of the query evaluation procedure is $O(n^2)$, where n is the number of tuples.

Soliman et al. [2010a] have also shown that when the score densities of individual tuples f_i's are uniform, weak stochastic transitivity always holds. Moreover, for two tuples, t_i, t_j, the test of $(\Pr(t_i > t_j) \geq 0.5)$ can be done more efficiently using the expected scores of t_i and t_j, as given by the following rule:

$$For \ uniform \ f_i, f_j : \mathrm{E}[f_i] \geq \mathrm{E}[f_j]) \Leftrightarrow (\Pr(t_i > t_j) \geq 0.5)$$

The previous rule allows a more efficient algorithm for computing the optimal rank aggregation in a PPO with uniform score densities. The algorithm is simply sorting tuples based on their expected scores, which results in the same sorting based on $\Pr(t_i > t_j)$ values, based on the previous rule. Computing $\mathrm{E}[f_i]$ for every tuple, t_i requires a linear scan over all tuples, which has a complexity of $O(n)$, while the subsequent sorting step has a complexity of $O(n\log(n))$. It follows that the query evaluation procedure has an overall complexity of $O(n\log(n))$.

Computing Rank Aggregation on Partial Lists We describe the algorithms proposed by Li and Deshpande [2009] to compute optimal aggregation of top-k lists, based on the definitions of distance functions given in Section 3.2.

Let $\mathcal{T} = \{\tau_1, \ldots, \tau_m\}$ be the set of possible k-prefixes (top-k vectors of possible worlds) of a relation R of n tuples $\{t_1, \ldots, t_n\}$ under the tuple uncertainty model. Let $r(t)$ be a random variable denoting the rank of tuple t in the space of possible k-prefixes. The results given by Li and Deshpande [2009] show that the optimal top-k aggregation under the Symmetric Difference distance function Δ is given by the k tuples with the largest UTop-Rank$(1, k)$ probabilities (this is the same as the k most probable tuples in the answer of PT-k query). The previous result follows by computing the expected distance between a permutation τ of k tuples and the possible k-prefixes. Note that, based on possible worlds semantics, the summation of the probabilities of tuples to appear at rank i is 1, which implies that $\sum_{t \in R} \Pr(r(t) \leq k) = k$. Hence, the expected distance between τ and a k-prefix τ_i can be derived as follows:

$$
\begin{aligned}
E[\Delta(\tau, \tau_i)] &= \sum_{\tau_i \in T} \Pr(\tau_i) \cdot \left(\sum_{t \in \tau \wedge t \notin \tau_i} 1 + \sum_{t \in \tau_i \wedge t \notin \tau} 1 \right) \\
&= \sum_{t \in \tau} \Pr(\neg t \vee r(t) > k) + \sum_{t \notin \tau} \Pr(r(t) \leq k) \\
&= \sum_{t \in \tau} 1 - \Pr(r(t) \leq k) + \sum_{t \notin \tau} \Pr(r(t) \leq k) \\
&= (k - \sum_{t \in \tau} \Pr(r(t) \leq k)) + (\sum_{t \in R} \Pr(r(t) \leq k) - \sum_{t \in \tau} \Pr(r(t) \leq k)) \\
&= 2k - 2 \sum_{t \in \tau} \Pr(r(t) \leq k)
\end{aligned}
$$

The previous derivation shows that $E[\Delta(\tau, \tau_i)]$ is minimized when the second term in the last equation is maximized, which implies that τ is given by the k tuples with the largest UTop-Rank$(1, k)$ probabilities.

Finding the optimal top-k aggregation under the Intersection and Extended Footrule distance functions (Section 3.2) have been shown by Li and Deshpande [2009] to be equivalent to instances of the bipartite graph matching problem (similar to our discussion in optimal aggregation of full lists), which can be solved in polynomial time.

CHAPTER 5

Uncertain Rank Join

In this chapter, we discuss handling uncertain scores when computing rank join queries. This discussion is based on the work of Soliman et al. [2010b]. We present in Section 5.1 a formulation for rank join queries on uncertain data. We give in Section 5.2 an uncertain rank join algorithm and show how it can be implemented as a pipelined query operator. We discuss integrating join operation with probabilistic ranking in Section 5.3.

5.1   UNCERTAIN RANK JOIN PROBLEM

We assume a process that joins a number of input relations based on a given deterministic join condition (e.g., join hotel and restaurant relations based on the traveling distance being smaller than 1 mile). That is, given a set of input tuples (one from each input relation), the join condition evaluates to either true or false. The result is a set of output tuples representing all the join results (e.g., hotel-restaurant joined tuples). For each join result, a score is computed based on a user-defined scoring function $\mathcal{F}$ (e.g., hotel.stars+restaurant.rating). The scoring function is assumed to be a monotone function (i.e., $\mathcal{F}(x_1, \ldots, x_n) \geq \mathcal{F}(\acute{x}_1, \ldots, \acute{x}_n)$ whenever $x_i \geq \acute{x}_i$ for every i). Typical scoring functions, such as summation, multiplication, min, max, and average, are monotone functions. We are interested in obtaining the k join results that maximize the value of $\mathcal{F}$.

When the scoring function $\mathcal{F}$ is defined on deterministic attributes, the top-k join results are obtained by sorting the join results on $\mathcal{F}$ and returning the top-k results. Many top-k join techniques [Ilyas et al., 2004a, Natsev et al., 2001] address the interaction between computing the join results and producing the top-k answers. The main insight of these methods is exploiting pre-sorted input relations as well as the scoring function monotonicity to avoid complete sorting of the join results before producing the top-k joins.

We consider a different variant of the problem where the scoring function $\mathcal{F}$ is defined on uncertain attributes, and hence there is a space of possible rankings of the join results. The objective is to integrate the join operation with the computation of a ranking of join results under the query semantics in Chapter 3. We start by formulating the uncertain rank join problem under the score uncertainty model described in Section 2.2.2.

Definition 5.1   **[Uncertain Rank Join (URankJoin)]** Let $\mathcal{R}$ be a set of relations $\{R_1, \ldots, R_m\}$, $\mathcal{F}: R_1 \bowtie \cdots \bowtie R_m \rightarrow \mathcal{I}$ be a monotone scoring function, where $\mathcal{I}$ is the domain of all possible sub-intervals of $[0,1]$, and k be an integer $\leq |R_1 \bowtie \cdots \bowtie R_m|$. The query URankJoin$(\mathcal{R}, \mathcal{F}, k)$ computes a total order ω^* under some probabilistic ranking semantics (described below) of tuples

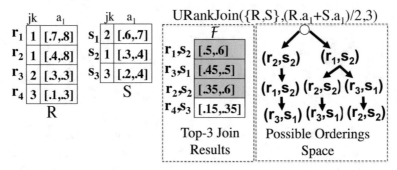

Figure 5.1: URankJoin example

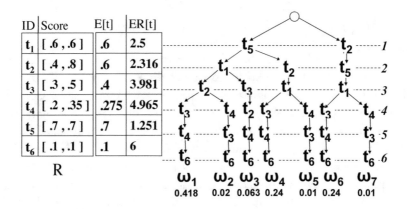

Figure 5.2: Space of possible orderings for tuples with uniform scores

in the set $\mathcal{J}_k \subseteq R_1 \bowtie \cdots \bowtie R_m$, where $|\mathcal{J}_k| \geq k$, and
$\forall t_i \in \mathcal{J}_k : |\{t_j \in R_1 \bowtie \cdots \bowtie R_m : t_j > t_i\}| < k$, and
$\forall t_j \notin \mathcal{J}_k : |\{t_i \in \mathcal{J}_k : t_i > t_j\}| \geq k$.   □

That is, URankJoin returns an ordering of tuples that have less than k other dominating tuples. To illustrate, consider Figure 5.1. URankJoin($\{R, S\}$, $(R.a_1 + S.a_1)/2$, 3), where the join condition is equality of attribute 'jk', returns a total order of join tuples in $\mathcal{J}_3 = \{(r_1, s_2), (r_3, s_1), (r_2, s_2)\}$, since all join tuples in $\mathcal{J}_3$ are dominated by less than 3 join tuples, and all join tuples not in $\mathcal{J}_3$ (only (r_4, s_3) in this example) are dominated by at least 3 tuples. Based on the monotonicity of $\mathcal{F}$, the *lo* and *up* scores of join tuples are given by applying $\mathcal{F}$ to the *lo* and *up* scores of the corresponding base tuples. For example, the score of (r_1, s_2) is given by $[\mathcal{F}(.7, .3), \mathcal{F}(.8, .4)] = [\frac{.7+.3}{2}, \frac{.8+.4}{2}] = [.5, .6]$.

Computing $\mathcal{J}_k$ does not require knowledge of f_i's of base or join tuples since $\mathcal{J}_k$ is based on score dominance only. However, computing ω^* requires knowledge of f_i's.

Let Ω be the set of all possible orderings of tuples in $\mathcal{J}_k$, and let $\omega[t]$ be the rank of t in an ordering $\omega \in \Omega$. An intuitive requirement in the total order ω^* is that it complies with score dominance (i.e., $(t_i > t_j) \Rightarrow (\omega^*[t_i] < \omega^*[t_j])$). To illustrate, consider Figure 5.2, which shows a relation R with uniform uncertain scores. The relation R has 7 possible orderings $\{\omega_1, \ldots, \omega_7\}$. Similar to the semantics discussed in Chapter 3, multiple query semantics can be adopted to order tuples in $\mathcal{J}_k$ in a way complying with score dominance. We list some examples of these semantics in the following:

(1) Expected Scores. Let $E[t_i] = \int_{lo_i}^{up_i} x \cdot f_i(x) dx$. Then, $\omega^*[t_i] = 1 + |\{t_j : E[t_j] > E[t_i]\}|$, while resolving ties deterministically. For example, in Figure 5.2, based on expected scores, $\omega^* = \langle t_5, t_1, t_2, t_3, t_4, t_6 \rangle$, assuming that the tie between t_1 and t_2 is resolved in favor of t_1.

(2) Expected Ranks. Let $ER[t_i] = \sum_{\omega \in \Omega} \omega[t_i] \cdot \Pr(\omega)$. Then, $\omega^*[t_i] = 1 + |\{t_j : ER[t_j] < ER[t_i]\}|$, while resolving ties deterministically. In Figure 5.2, based on expected ranks, $\omega^* = \langle t_5, t_2, t_1, t_3, t_4, t_6 \rangle$. The same definition is used by Cormode et al. [2009] with the addition that tuples can be excluded from some orderings due to their membership uncertainty.

(3) Most Probable Ordering. Similar to the UTop-Prefix query semantics in Definition 3.1, ω^* is defined as $argmax_{\omega \in \Omega} \Pr(\omega)$, where $\Pr(\omega)$ is computed using Equation 2.2. For example, in Figure 5.2, ω^* is the ordering $\omega_1 = \langle t_5, t_1, t_2, t_3, t_4, t_6 \rangle$.

5.2 COMPUTING THE TOP-K JOIN RESULTS

Current rank join methods [Ilyas et al., 2004b, Natsev et al., 2001, Schnaitter and Polyzotis, 2008] build on using sorted inputs to incrementally report ranked join results by bounding the scores of non-materialized join results. The proposed techniques mainly differ in the maintained state of partial joins (i.e., joins that may lead to valid join results), which can either be a lightweight state that gives loose score bounds [Ilyas et al., 2004b], or a dense state, of all partial joins that gives tight score bounds [Schnaitter and Polyzotis, 2008]. The scoring model in all of these methods is deterministic (i.e., each record has a single score), and hence they cannot be applied to settings with uncertain scores.

The objective of top-k queries is to produce the set of top-ranked tuples based on computed scores. Under the attribute level uncertainty model in Section 2.2, tuples dominated by $\geq k$ tuples can be safely pruned from the answer space of top-k queries. We would like to integrate the join operation with such k-dominance criterion such that we produce top-k join results as early as possible. In the following, we describe how to compute and sort join results incrementally (as needed) using a rank join algorithm that early prunes all dominated tuples.

A common interface to most rank join algorithms is to assume input relations sorted on per-relation scores, while output (join) relation is generated incrementally in join scores order. We show how to use a generic rank join algorithm RJ, complying with the previous interface, as a building block to compute $\mathcal{J}_k$ (the set of join results dominated by less than k join results) incrementally.

Algorithm Compute-$\mathcal{J}_k$ (described in Algorithm 4) assumes two sorted inputs (e.g., indexes), L_{lo}^i and L_{up}^i, for each input relation R_i, giving relation tuples ordered on lo and up scores, respectively.

Algorithm 4 Compute Top-k Join Results   [Soliman et al., 2010b]

Compute-$\mathcal{J}_k(L_{lo}^1, L_{up}^1, \ldots, L_{lo}^m, L_{up}^m$:Ranked Inputs, k:Answer Size, $\mathcal{F}$:Scoring Function)

  1   $RJ_{lo} \leftarrow$ an instance of RJ $(L_{lo}^1, \ldots, L_{lo}^m, k, \mathcal{F})$

  2   $RJ_{up} \leftarrow$ an instance of RJ $(L_{up}^1, \ldots, L_{up}^m, \infty, \mathcal{F})$

  3   $active_{lo} \leftarrow$ TRUE ; $active_{up} \leftarrow$ TRUE

  4   $T_{up} \leftarrow 1$ {*initialize score upper bound in RJ_{up}*}

  5   *count* $\leftarrow 0$ {*number of results reported by RJ_{lo}*}

  6   **while** ($active_{lo}$ OR $active_{up}$) **do**

  7   **if** ($active_{lo}$) **then**

  8       $t \leftarrow$ get next result from RJ_{lo}

  9   *count* $\leftarrow$ *count* $+ 1$

10   **if** (*count* $= k$) **then** $active_{lo} \leftarrow$ FALSE

11       $T_{lo} \leftarrow$ score of t

12   **while** ($T_{up} > T_{lo}$) **do**

13   Report results available in RJ_{up} with scores $> T_{lo}$

14       $T_{up} \leftarrow$ score upper bound in RJ_{up}

15   **if** (NOT $active_{lo}$ AND $T_{up} < T_{lo}$) **then**

16       $active_{up} \leftarrow$ FALSE

By processing the *lo* and *up* inputs simultaneously, Compute-$\mathcal{J}_k$ incrementally computes $\mathcal{J}_k$. This is done by using two instances of RJ, denoted RJ_{lo} and RJ_{up}, where RJ_{lo} rank-joins tuples on their overall *lo* scores to find exactly k join results, while RJ_{up} rank-joins tuples on their overall *up* scores to find all join results with *up* scores above the kth largest score reported by RJ_{lo}. The execution of RJ_{lo} and RJ_{up} is interleaved, such that, at any point during execution, RJ_{up} reports all tuples whose *up* scores are above the last *lo* score reported by RJ_{lo}. Tuples in $\mathcal{J}_k$ are reported in *up* scores order to allow for incremental ranking (cf. Section 5.3).

Pipelined Operator. Pipelined URankJoin query plans requires wrapping Compute-$\mathcal{J}_k$ into a query operator. For clarity of presentation, we focus on 2-way joins plans. However, the techniques we discuss can also handle multi-way joins. A pipelined operator implementation of Compute-$\mathcal{J}_k$ requires making the algorithm independent of k. The knowledge of k is only available to the query plan root that drives plan execution, while the operator only responds to incoming requests of join results ordered on either *lo* or *up* scores.

    A URankJoin plan is rooted by ULIMIT, an operator driving URankJoin plan execution. We describe the operator's implementation of the iterator model in Algorithm 5. The operator takes two inputs, I_{lo} and I_{up}, representing two streams of query output tuples ordered on their *lo* scores and *up* scores, respectively. One GetNext implementation is to consume k tuples from I_{lo} and to

---

Algorithm 5 ULIMIT Operator [Soliman et al., 2010b]

Open(I_{lo}: lo input stream, I_{up}: up input stream, k: Answer Size)

1   I_{lo}.Open()
2   I_{up}.Open()
3   $\overline{\mathcal{F}_{lo}} \leftarrow 1.0$
4   $count \leftarrow 0$

GetNext()

1   **while** ($count < k$) **do**
2       $t \leftarrow I_{lo}$.GetNext()
3       $count \leftarrow count + 1$
4   **if** ($count = k$) **then** $\overline{\mathcal{F}_{lo}} \leftarrow lo$ score of t
5   $t \leftarrow I_{up}$.GetNext()
6   **if** (up score of $t > \overline{\mathcal{F}_{lo}}$) **then return** t **else return** null

Close()

1   I_{lo}.Close()
2   I_{up}.Close()

---

report tuples in I_{up} with scores above the kth score in I_{lo}. An alternative GetNext implementation is to interleave drawing tuples from I_{lo} and I_{up}, similar to Algorithm Compute-$\mathcal{J}_k$.

A URankJoin operator is a logical operator that accepts two inputs; each has two sorted access paths, corresponding to the lo and up score orders of the two input relations. The operator produces two output tuple streams corresponding to sorted join results based on lo and up scores.

Figure 5.3 gives an example logical URankJoin query plan. The shown plan rank-joins three relations R, S, and T with uncertain scores x, y, and z, respectively. The bottom URankJoin operator uses indexes on the lo and up scores in Relations R and S as its input access paths, while the top URankJoin operator uses indexes on Relation T and the output of the bottom URankJoin operator as its input access paths. The ULIMIT operator consumes both lo and up inputs from the top URankJoin operator.

URankJoin operator can have different physical implementation. One implementation is to use two regular rank join operators wrapped within a physical operator with 4 inputs (the lo and up orders of the two input relations) and 2 outputs (the lo and up orders of the join results). This implementation requires, however, making other query operators aware of the URankJoin operator input/output interface. An alternative implementation is to use two separate rank join operators, which allows building URankJoin plan as two parallel plans that can be optimized independently based on available data access paths.

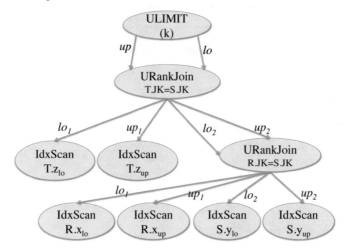

Figure 5.3: A logical URankJoin query plan

5.3   RANKING THE TOP-K JOIN RESULTS

A major challenge for ordering tuples with uncertain scores is managing the exponentially large space of possible orderings (cf. Section 2.2). For the uncertain rank join problem, this challenge is tackled using a sampling-based infrastructure for computing ω^* under multiple semantics based on two techniques: *Join-aware Sampling* and *Incremental Ranking*.

5.3.1   JOIN-AWARE SAMPLING

Join induces dependencies among join results. For example, in Figure 5.1, (r_1, s_2) and (r_2, s_2) are dependent since they originate from one tuple $s_2 \in S$ and different tuples in R. Such dependency means that the joint score density of (r_1, s_2) and (r_2, s_2) (which produces the probability of any ordering involving (r_1, s_2) and (r_2, s_2)) is not given by multiplying the marginal score densities of (r_1, s_2) and (r_2, s_2). That is, the score random variables of (r_1, s_2) and (r_2, s_2) are dependent.

Score dependencies are handled by associating join results with lineage representing the keys of their origin base tuples. The main idea is to use the space with independent score random variables (i.e., base tuples) as a generator of the space with dependent score random variables (i.e., join results). Hence, the probability of an ordering of (possibly dependent) join results is computed using independent samples drawn from the space of base scores.

Figure 5.4 illustrates the previous approach. The set $\mathcal{J}_3$ is produced by the URankJoin query in Figure 5.1. Each join result in $\mathcal{J}_3$ is associated with the keys of its origin base tuples. To compute $\Pr(\langle t_1, t_2, t_3 \rangle)$, we independently sample a score value in each origin base tuple of $\mathcal{J}_3$ (i.e., a score value in each of $\{r_1, r_2, r_3, s_1, s_2\}$). We simply call such vector of base tuples' score samples a *base sample*. Since base tuple scores are independent, the probability of each base sample is the product

$\mathcal{F}$	Lineage
t_1 [.5,.6]	r_1,s_2
t_2 [.45,.5]	r_3,s_1
t_3 [.35,.6]	r_2,s_2

$\mathcal{J}_3$

Avg(.73,.4)

Samples		Source Base Tuples					Join Tuples			
		r_1	r_2	r_3	s_1	s_2	t_1	t_2	t_3	
	1	.73	.5	.3	.65	.4	.565	.475	.45	✓
	2	.78	.42	.3	.6	.35	.565	.45	.385	✓
	3	.72	.72	.3	.67	.33	.525	.485	.525	
	4	.75	.78	.3	.62	.31	.53	.46	.545	
	5	.77	.45	.3	.64	.38	.575	.47	.415	✓

Monte-Carlo sampling to compute $\Pr(\langle t_1,t_2,t_3 \rangle)$

Figure 5.4: Handling score dependencies in Monte-Carlo sampling

of the probabilities of its constituent score values. Applying $\mathcal{F}$ (the average) to score values in a base sample gives a score sample for each join results in $\mathcal{J}_3$. We mark, in Figure 5.4, the base samples that correspond to the ordering $\langle t_1, t_2, t_3 \rangle$. Such base samples are called *hits*.

Algorithm 6 shows how to use the Monte-Carlo method to compute $\Pr(\omega)$, where ω is an ordering of join results (cf. Section 5.3). The union of the lineage of join results in ω is first computed. Independent samples are drawn from the score distributions of base tuples included in the lineage. The drawn scores produce an ordering of join results. If such ordering agrees with ω, then the sample is a *hit*. The probabilities of hits corresponding to join results ordering ω are averaged when using Monte-Carlo integration method to compute $\Pr(\omega)$.

We show how to use the previous infrastructure to compute the total order ω^* of tuples in $\mathcal{J}_k$ under *expected ranks* semantics.

The expected rank of a tuple t_i $(ER(t_i))$ is computed as $\sum_{\omega \in \Omega} \Pr(\omega) \cdot \omega[t_i]$ (cf. Section 5.1). Computing $ER(t_i)$ can be done efficiently by rewriting $ER(t_i)$ as $\sum_{r=1}^{|\mathcal{J}_k|} r \cdot \Pr(t_i, r)$, where $\Pr(t_i, r)$ is the probability of t_i to be at rank r in the possible orderings of $\mathcal{J}_k$. The correctness of the previous rewrite follows from the fact that $\Pr(t_i, r) = \sum_{\omega_{(t_i,r)} \in \Omega} \Pr(\omega_{(t_i,r)})$, where $\omega_{(t_i,r)}$ has t_i at rank r.

We compute $\Pr(t_i, r)$ by considering as a *hit* each sample of base scores that results in the join tuple t_i being at rank r. For example, in Figure 5.4, to compute $\Pr(t_3, 1)$, we consider sample 3 and sample 4 as *hits*.

We describe how to compute an ordering ω^* of join results under other probabilistic ranking semantics:

(1) The Most Probable Ordering. In Section 4.2.2, we discussed using Markov Chains Monte-Carlo (MCMC) methods to approximate the most probable ordering by drawing samples from the orderings space biased by probability. The main idea is that for a current sample (ordering) ω_i, and a newly proposed sample ω_{i+1}, we always accept ω_{i+1} if $\Pr(\omega_{i+1}) > \Pr(\omega_i)$; otherwise, we accept ω_{i+1} with probability proportional to $\Pr(\omega_{i+1})/\Pr(\omega_i)$. The MCMC method provably converges

---

Algorithm 6 Compute Probability of Join Results Ordering   [Soliman et al., 2010b]

MC-Probability(ω: Join results ordering, s: Number of samples)

1   $sources \leftarrow \bigcup_{t \in \omega} t.sources$ {*compute lineage of ω*}

2   $hits \leftarrow 0$ {*no. of samples matching ordering given by ω*}

3   $sum \leftarrow 0$ {*summation of hits probabilities*}

4   **for** $i = 1$ to s **do**

5       $sample \leftarrow [\ ]$ {*a sample of the scores of base tuples*}

6   **for** each tuple $t_i \in sources$ **do**

7           $sample[t_i.key] \leftarrow$ random score value based on f_i

8       $\acute{\omega} \leftarrow$ ordering of join tuples based on base scores in $sample$

9   **if** ($\acute{\omega}$ agrees with the tuple ordering given by ω) **then**

10          $hits \leftarrow hits + 1$

11          $sum \leftarrow sum + \Pi_{z \in sample}(\text{Pr}(z))$

12      $v \leftarrow$ volume of hypercube enclosing score combinations in ω

13 **return** $\frac{hits}{s} \cdot v \cdot \frac{sum}{hits}$

---

to the target distribution of possible orderings, and hence it can be used as a generator of orderings biased by their probabilities. Algorithm 6 allows computing $\text{Pr}(\omega)$, where ω is an ordering of join results, and hence applying the MCMC method to approximate the most probable ordering.

(2) Other Semantics. Computing $\text{Pr}(t_i, r)$ allows computing ω^* under other probabilistic ranking semantics. For example, tuple's probability to appear at the top ranks only (Global Top-k [Zhang and Chomicki, 2009]) is computed as $\text{Pr}_k(t_i) = \sum_{r=1}^{k} \text{Pr}(t_i, r)$. Similarly, pruning tuples whose probabilities to appear at the top ranks is below a given threshold (probabilistic Top-k threshold [Hua et al., 2008]) can be done by testing if $\text{Pr}_k(t_i) < T$, for a given threshold T. A third example is finding the ordering with the minimum disagreements with other orderings in the space (Uncertain Rank Aggregation), which can be done in polynomial time using $\text{Pr}(t_i, r)$ values as shown in Section 4.4.2.

5.3.2   INCREMENTAL RANKING

The size of $\mathcal{J}_k$ can be much larger than k due to score uncertainty. In many Web application scenarios, users only inspect a small prefix of the ranked answers list (e.g., inspecting only a few top hits returned by a search engine). Computing a full ranking of all answers in advance may not thus be always required. We discuss using the incremental computation of $\mathcal{J}_k$ (cf. Section 5.2) to incrementally compute an approximation of ω^*.

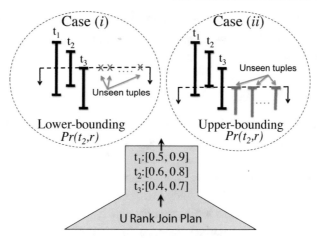

Figure 5.5: Bounding $\Pr(t_2, i)$

The main idea is computing bounds on $\Pr(t_i, r)$ for each join result t_i produced by a URankJoin plan. The bounds of $\Pr(t_i, r)$ are used to approximate a prefix of ω^*, and they are progressively tightened as more tuples are produced by the URankJoin plan.

Figure 5.5 shows a URankJoin plan that produces tuples in $\mathcal{J}_k$ ordered on their *up* scores. The last produced tuple at this step is t_3. Assume that we need to compute $\Pr(t_2, r)$. We identify two extreme cases:

- Case (i): the scores of all non-retrieved tuples are deterministic values (shown as '×' symbols in Figure 5.5) located at the largest possible unseen score (i.e., up_3).

- Case (ii): the *up* scores of all non-retrieved tuples are below lo_2 (shown as shaded intervals in Figure 5.5).

Each case gives a possible configuration of unseen tuples in $\mathcal{J}_k$. By applying Monte-Carlo sampling to each configuration, we obtain a bound on $\Pr(t_2, r)$. Specifically, Case (i) gives a lower bound on $\Pr(t_2, r)$, denoted $\Pr^\downarrow(t_2, r)$, since the scores of all unseen tuples are maximized, while Case (ii) gives an upper bound on $\Pr(t_2, r)$, denoted $\Pr^\uparrow(t_2, r)$, since the scores of all unseen tuples are minimized. By seeing more tuples in $\mathcal{J}_k$, computed bounds are tightened (i.e., $\Pr^\downarrow(t_2, r)$ increases and $\Pr^\uparrow(t_2, r)$ decreases) since the maximum score of an unseen tuple decreases. When the maximum score of an unseen tuple is below lo_2, both bounds coincide at $\Pr(t_2, r)$. Note that this bounding method is valid only if tuples in $\mathcal{J}_k$ are retrieved in *up* score order.

The bounds of $\Pr(t_i, r)$ can be used to compute rankings under multiple probabilistic ranking semantics. For example, in Global top-k [Zhang and Chomicki, 2009], $\Pr_k(t_i)$ can be bounded as $\Pr_k{}^\downarrow(t_i) = \sum_{r=1}^{k} \Pr^\downarrow(t_i, r)$, and $\Pr_k{}^\uparrow(t_i) = \min(1, \sum_{r=1}^{k} \Pr^\uparrow(t_i, r))$. The Global top-$k$ ranking of retrieved tuples from $\mathcal{J}_k$ can thus be approximated as follows. We set $\omega^*[t_i] < \omega^*[t_j]$ if $\Pr_k{}^\downarrow(t_i) >$

$\Pr_k{}^\uparrow(t_j) - \epsilon$, where $\epsilon \in [0, 1)$ is a given acceptable error in tuples relative order. The underlying URankJoin plan is incrementally requested for new join results until the computed ω^* prefix satisfies the previous error constraint.

5.4   MASHRANK PROTOTYPE

We describe the architecture of MashRank [Soliman et al., 2010b], a research prototype that applies uncertain rank join techniques, discussed in this chapter, in the context of data mashups on the Web.

Current mashup systems allow creating data flows involving services, sources, and operators. Most systems assume data in the form of pre-computed structured feeds, with the exception of the proposal of Simmen, D. et al [2009], which integrates text extractors into enterprise mashups. However, ranking is mostly overlooked in these works which only consider unoptimized plans (e.g., materialze-sort plans) for processing ranked mashups. Moreover, although uncertainty is ubiquitous on the Web (e.g., missing/inexact values), current systems do not allow querying/reasoning about such uncertainty. The MashRank prototype integrates concepts from information extraction, rank-aware processing, and probabilistic databases domains to address these problems.

5.4.1   MASHRANK ARCHITECTURE

MashRank is a Web-accessible system [1] with client-side query processing, and server-side data retrieval and information extraction. We describe the details of different components in MashRank architecture (given in Figure 5.6).

Mashup Editor   builds a mashup data flow, by interacting with the user, to identify source schemas, join/filter conditions, and scoring function. A mashup data flow is a tree whose leaves are the sources, and internal nodes are three primary logical operators: extractors, joins, and filters. The edges between tree nodes are pipes indicating the flow of tuples from one logical operator to its parent.

Mashup Planner   maps the mashup data flow into a rank-aware and uncertainty-aware physical plan. A mashup physical plan needs to be rank-aware if the user provides a scoring function to order mashup results. The physical plan needs to be uncertainty-aware if the scoring function involves at least one uncertain attribute.

Mashup Planner exploits sorting capabilities of input sources to offload sort to source side. For example, if the scoring function involves an attribute that has sorted access (as provided by its corresponding source), the created mashup plan pushes source records directly (i.e., without a sorting phase) into rank-aware mashup execution. This also allows limiting extraction on pages that are not required to compute the top-ranked results (by upper bounding the scores of records not yet extracted). We elaborate on planning and sort offloading in Section 5.4.3.

Figure 5.7 shows an example mashup data flow, constructed using MashRank editor, a corresponding mashup physical join plan, and a listing of computed mashup results.

---

[1]Prototype is accessible at `http://prefex.cs.uwaterloo.ca/MashRank` (accessed on December 28, 2010)

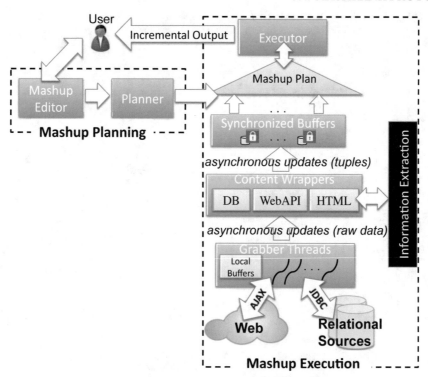

Figure 5.6: MashRank architecture

Content Wrappers   bridge different data models to the relational model. Mashups may involve data sources of different models (e.g., XML generated by Web API's, raw HTML, and relational data). MashRank adopts a simple relational model in which mashup (intermediate) results are represented as tuples.

Wrapping HTML into relational tuples is complicated by the lacking of schema information. MashRank builds HTML wrappers based on the concepts of *wrapper induction* [Kushmerick, N., 1997] in information extraction. The idea is to request user to provide a number of labeled examples of different attributes in a sample of source pages. A wrapper inductor learns a rule that correctly extracts all of the given examples. For example, the rule can be maximal strings in HTML source that delimit all of the examples. Applying the rule to other source pages, with the same structure of labeled pages, produces the required tuples. We elaborate on wrapper induction details in Section 5.4.2

Grabber Threads   grab data from mashup sources. When sources are accessible through URLs, MashRank initiates a thread for each URL to grab contents. Each thread forwards source response, once ready, to the appropriate wrapper. This allows MashRank to process multiple requests in parallel,

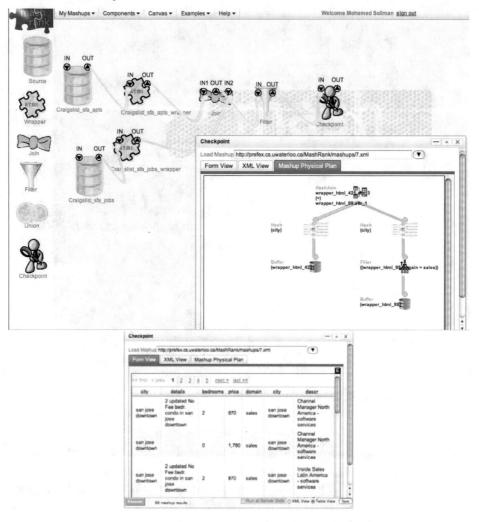

Figure 5.7: A Screenshot for MashRank prototype

and avoid getting blocked on slow sources. When sources are relational, a database connection is used to retrieve tuples from remote database.

Mashup Executor   executes the physical plan generated by the Planner against live data sources, and incrementally reports mashup results to the user. MashRank builds on the iterator model (Open-GetNext-Close), used in most DBMS, for mashup execution. Opening the root operator in a query plan tree recursively initializes all tree operators. Processing the query is done by calling the GetNext method of the root operator repeatedly until it returns an empty result. Finally, Closing the root operator recursively shuts down all operators in the tree.

However, in contrast to relational plans that read data from tables with known sizes residing on disks, a mashup plan may read data from remote sources of unknown sizes filling up asynchronously as more tuples are extracted. Hence, mashup execution needs to be (1) *synchronized*: to guarantee correct reads/updates, sources are locked when wrappers attempt to append new extracted tuples, or when parent nodes in the mashup plan attempt to read next tuple; and (2) *push-based*: an operator requesting tuples waits if no new tuples are currently available, and wrappers are not done processing source contents. Once new records are available, they are pushed into plan execution by notifying all waiting requesters.

Each mashup source has a dedicated *synchronized buffer* satisfying these two requirements. Synchronized buffer owns a monitor (lock) to prevent concurrent reads and updates. Wrappers writing to the buffer, as well as mashup plan nodes, reading from the buffer, must obtain buffer's lock before accessing its data. If a read/write request is being served, all other requests are forced to wait until the request being served completes. As soon as the request completes, a notification message is issued to wake up all waiting requests to re-attempt accessing the buffer.

MashRank executor interleaves extraction with query processing such that none of the two tasks blocks the other. Moreover, variance in source response times is tolerated by allowing asynchronous updates as soon as source responds with contents, as opposed to blocking until source responds. Hence, the execution is geared toward early-out of mashup results, if possible, while extraction and query processing are in progress.

5.4.2   INFORMATION EXTRACTION

Information extraction techniques approach unstructured data from different perspectives. Supervised learning methods [Kushmerick, N., 1997], learn extraction rules from a set of user-specified examples by generalizing common properties in these examples. On the other hand, unsupervised learning methods [Crescenzi, V., 2001] focus on learning a grammar/template describing the schema of the underlying source by exploiting repeated structure and domain knowledge. The learned template can be used to populate relational tables out of the unstructured sources. MashRank provides a mashup authoring tool that builds on supervised extraction methods, namely wrapper induction. Users are allowed to annotate and refine examples, during mashup data flow creation, and use these examples to learn extraction rules. In the following, we present an adaptation of wrapper induction techniques to accomplish such a task.

MashRank uses wrapper induction techniques to transform unstructured sources into relational (structured) sources. The details of the wrapper induction algorithm are orthogonal to mashup planning and processing in MashRank. An interface is assumed to the wrapper inductor with three main functions: (1) *addExample*: adds a new training example (e.g., a text node representing the value of some attribute); (2) *learn*: processes the training examples using the induction algorithm to compute an extraction rule; and (3) *extract*: applies the learned extraction rule to a given page, and returns a set of extracted records.

The previous interface is generic, and applies to multiple wrapper induction proposals. We elaborate on the implementation of the previous interface in an adaptation of the proposal of Kushmerick, N. [1997]. The inductor proposed by Kushmerick, N. [1997] treats each HTML page as a sequence of characters, and learns extraction rules in the form of string patterns. The learned rule extracts attributes from the page source in a round-robin fashion, and binds them into records. This method can generate erroneous records when some attribute values are missing. Since missing values are common on the Web, this method is adapted by learning extraction rules on attribute level, and then bind extracted values into records based on their proximity in the HTML source. We describe this technique in the following.

For a schema $\langle a_1, \ldots, a_n \rangle$ of n attributes, the function *addExample* receives as input a triple (a_i, s, e), where a_i is a schema attribute, while s and e are the start and end character positions of one example value of a_i in the HTML source. In MashRank editor, this is enabled by allowing the user to highlight pieces of text inside the page as examples for each required attribute.

The function *learn* computes an extraction rule for each attribute a_i in the form of a pair of strings (l_i, r_i). The rule is interpreted as follows: all values of attribute a_i appearing in the underlying page are enclosed between two strings l_i and r_i. For example, one possible extraction rule for hotel name could simply be (" $< b >$", " $< /b >$"). The strings l_i and r_i are computed by scanning the characters appearing before and after all training examples, and appending these characters to l_i and r_i, respectively, as long as all examples agree on the scanned character. We stop when finding maximal patterns in the sense that by appending more characters to any of l_i and r_i, at least one training example is not matched.

The function *extract* applies the extraction rule of each attribute to extract a set of attribute values. We align extracted values to form records based on their proximity in the page. We process attributes in the order in which they appear in the HTML source (e.g., *name* appears before *price*), and within each attribute, we process extracted values in the order of their appearance in the HTML source. We start by assigning each extracted value in the first attribute to a new record. For each subsequent attribute a_i, we assign attribute value v to the record that has an attribute a_j, with $j < i$, whose value is the closest value preceding v. If such record cannot be found, v is assigned to a new record with empty values in all attributes a_j for $j < i$, and value v in attribute a_i.

5.4.3 MASHUP PLANNING

Query optimizers use statistics collected on queried relations, and query predicates, to prune query plans that are expected to perform poorly. In mashup settings, we usually have no prior knowledge about data sources, as they may be remote sources given by the user in an ad-hoc fashion. MashRank resorts to exploiting the configuration of mashup data flow to build a feasible mashup physical plan. Nevertheless, building mashup planning on a cost model can be quite important in many other scenarios (e.g., mashing up sources that the system has prior knowledge on, asking for user input to characterize cost factors of mashed up sources, or sampling the sources to compute estimates on their cost factors).

Given a ranked mashup with a scoring dunction $\mathcal{F}$, MashRank Planner starts by labeling each node in the mashup data flow with its corresponding ranking attributes (attributes that appear in $\mathcal{F}$). The labeling starts with leaves (data sources), where each source is labeled with the ranking attributes it covers. Then, moving up in the data flow tree, the union of the ranking attributes of all children of a node p gives the ranking attributes of p.

After labeling is done, the Planner processes the labeled data flow starting from the root, mapping each node to one or more physical operators, and then recursing on nodes' children.

A source node is mapped to a *synchronized buffer* (cf. Section 5.4.1). An extractor node with empty ranking attributes is mapped to a *scan* operator. An extractor node with non-empty ranking attributes is mapped to *sort* operator, on top of a *scan* operator, so that all source tuples are sorted based on the scoring function (ranking attributes not belonging to the source assume the largest possible score). Since we generally assume monotone scoring functions, using such sort expression guarantees tuples flowing out of the source in the right order. A join node with empty ranking attributes is mapped to either a *nested-loops join* operator, or a *hash join* operator if the join condition is non-equality or equality, respectively. Similarly, a join node with non-empty ranking attributes is mapped to a *nested-loops rank join* operator, or a *hash rank join* operator [2] if the join condition is non-equality or equality, respectively. Finally, a filter node is mapped to a *filter* operator with the node's Boolean condition.

When the scoring function includes one or more uncertain attributes, the Planner generates a URankJoin plan (cf. Section 5.2). The above procedure is followed to generate two identical rank join plans, where one plan rank-joins tuples on their *lo* scores, while the other plan rank-jons tuples on their *up* scores. A *ULimit* operator is used as the parent operator of the two plans, and a *probranker* operator (implementing MC-based sampling methods) is added as the parent of *ULimit*.

We describe the plan generation algorithm using the following rank join query:

```
SELECT *
FROM vianet, tvtrip
WHERE vianet.HotelName ~ tvtrip.HotelName
ORDER BY 500 - vianet.Price+ 100 * tvtrip.Rating
LIMIT k
```

where vianet and tvtrip are two Web sources providing hotel pricing and rating information, respectively. The scoring function includes two attributes *price*, and *rating*, where *price* is an uncertain attribute. The join condition is approximate equality of hotel names (implemented in MashRank as a thresholded edit distance similarity function). Figure 5.8 shows the data flow nodes after being

---

[2]The Hash Rank Join (HRJN) algorithm [Ilyas et al., 2004b] iteratively selects an input relation to read its next tuple. Each new tuple is hashed on its join attribute in a per-relation hash table to facilitate creating join results. The join results are created by finding, for each new tuple, the joinable tuples currently read from other relations. Join results are stored in a priority queue ordered on score. The scores of non-materialized join results are upper-bounded by assuming best-case joins, where tuples with the highest scores in all inputs, but one, join with the last retrieved tuple from the excluded input.

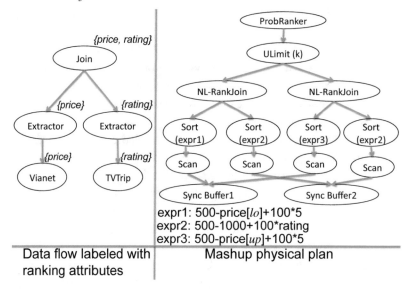

Figure 5.8: Generating mashup plan

labeled with ranking attributes. The generated physical plan is a nested-loops rank join plan (since join condition is non-equality). The Planner adds a *ULimit* operator to drive the execution of the *lo* and *up* rank join plans, and a *probranker* operator to conduct probabilistic ranking. The sort expressions ($expr_1$, $expr_2$, and $expr_3$) are created by replacing ranking attributes not covered by the underlying source with their largest possible scores.

Offloading Sort to Web Sources.   In rank-aware query processing, the existence of sorted access methods on ranking attributes is crucial for pipelining ranked results efficiently. Implementing such access methods as a sort operator per input (e.g., as in Figure 5.8) introduces a bottleneck in query execution due to the blocking nature of sort. When an index on a ranking attribute already exists, a rank-aware plan can benefit from such cheap sorted access method to pipeline ranked query results efficiently.

In mashup settings, we build on arbitrary sources selected by the user, and hence we cannot generally assume the existence of indexes on these sources. However, many Web sources provide sorting capabilities to view query results ordered on some attribute. Such information is obtained from the user in the form of a special sorting parameter that can be appended to page URLs. By offloading sort to source side, we allow rank-aware mashup plan to pipeline sorted results, as they are extracted from the sources.

For example, assume the following mashup query, where vianet is declared by the user as a source that can produce records ordered on *price_up* (the *up* values of *price* attribute):

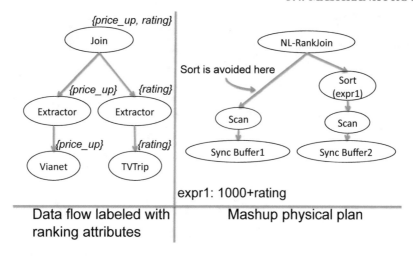

Figure 5.9: Generating mashup plan with offloaded sorting

```
SELECT *
FROM vianet, tvtrip
WHERE vianet.HotelName ~ tvtrip.HotelName
ORDER BY vianet.Price_up+ tvtrip.Rating
LIMIT k
```

Fiigure 5.9 shows the mashup data flow labeled with ranking attributes, and the corresponding physical plan generated by MashRank Planner. Note that the Planner did not add a sort on top of the scan of Vianet, since it leveraged the fact that records of Vianet are pre-sorted, and hence they can be directly pipelined into the NL-RankJoin operator.

Finally, we illustrate how the data grabbing module (cf. Section 5.4.1) exploits sorted access methods. The multi-threaded architecture of MashRank spawns a grabber thread per page to avoid blocking on slow sources. When each thread grabs data from one of the pages in a sorted retrieval, some of the pages can be ready for extraction before others, due to differences in source response time. We thus need to an maintain a page-level order to guarantee pipelining records into mashup execution in the right order. This is done by associating each thread with an order reflecting the position of the thread's page in the ordered retrieval of source pages. Tuple requests are answered while respecting such page-level order. That is, a tuple is not reported from page p unless all tuples in pages with orders preceding p have been already reported.

CHAPTER 6

Conclusion

This lecture compiles and summarizes state-of-the-art techniques supporting ranked retrieval in uncertain and probabilistic databases. The lecture discusses the interplay between ranking and uncertainty models, and it describes several proposed mechanisms to compute ranking queries under different types of data uncertainty.

We describe the uncertainty models adopted by current probabilistic ranking techniques and the assumptions made by these models. We also discuss multiple proposed query semantics and highlight their impact on the design of current probabilistic ranking proposals.

We illustrate the technical details of several query evaluation methods introduced by current probabilistic ranking proposals. We categorize these methods based on their adopted approaches and discuss multiple examples under each category. We also show how current proposals handle join queries in the context probabilistic ranking.

Bibliography

Serge Abiteboul, Paris Kanellakis, and Gosta Grahne. On the representation and querying of sets of possible worlds. *ACM SIGMOD Rec.*, 16(3):34–48, 1987. DOI: 10.1145/38714.38724 9

Periklis Andritsos, Ariel Fuxman, and Renee J. Miller. Clean answers over dirty databases: A probabilistic approach. In *Proc. 22nd Int. Conf. on Data Engineering*, page 30, 2006. DOI: 10.1109/ICDE.2006.35 9

Omar Benjelloun, Anish Das Sarma, Alon Halevy, and Jennifer Widom. Uldbs: Databases with uncertainty and lineage. In *Proc. 32nd Int. Conf. on Very Large Data Bases*, pages 953–964, 2006. 1, 9

Graham Brightwell and Peter Winkler. Counting linear extensions is #p-complete. In *Proc. 23rd Annual ACM Symp. on Theory of Computing*, pages 175–181, 1991. DOI: 10.1145/103418.103441 5

Chee-Yong Chan, H. V. Jagadish, Kian-Lee Tan, Anthony K. H. Tung, and Zhenjie Zhang. Finding k-dominant skylines in high dimensional space. In *Proc. ACM SIGMOD Int. Conf. on Management of Data*, pages 503–514, 2006. DOI: 10.1145/1142473.1142530 5

Reynold Cheng, Sunil Prabhakar, and Dmitri V. Kalashnikov. Querying imprecise data in moving object environments. In *Proc. 19th Int. Conf. on Data Engineering*, pages 723–725, 2003. DOI: 10.1109/TKDE.2004.46 5

Jan Chomicki. Preference formulas in relational queries. *ACM Trans. Database Syst.*, 28(4):427–466, 2003. DOI: 10.1145/958942.958946 4

G. Cormode, F. Li, and K. Yi. Semantics of ranking queries for probabilistic data and expected ranks. In *Proc. 25th Int. Conf. on Data Engineering*, pages 305–316, 2009. DOI: 10.1109/ICDE.2009.75 6, 22, 23, 42, 43, 49

Nilesh Dalvi and Dan Suciu. Efficient query evaluation on probabilistic databases. *VLDB J.*, 16(4): 523–544, 2007. DOI: 10.1007/s00778-006-0004-3 1, 9

Pedro Domingos and Daniel Lowd. *Markov Logic: An Interface Layer for Artificial Intelligence.* Morgan & Claypool Publishers, 2009. DOI: 10.2200/S00206ED1V01Y200907AIM007 12

Cynthia Dwork, Ravi Kumar, Moni Naor, and D. Sivakumar. Rank aggregation methods for the web. In *Proc. 10th Int. World Wide Web Conf.*, pages 613–622, 2001. DOI: 10.1145/371920.372165 26, 43, 44

Ronald Fagin, Ravi Kumar, and D. Sivakumar. Comparing top k lists. In *Proc. 14th Annual ACM-SIAM Symp. on Discrete Algorithms*, pages 28–36, 2003. 24

Tingjian Ge, Stan Zdonik, and Samuel Madden. Top-k queries on uncertain data: on score distribution and typical answers. In *Proc. ACM SIGMOD Int. Conf. on Management of Data*, pages 375–388, 2009. DOI: 10.1145/1559845.1559886 6, 24, 25, 26, 40, 41, 42

Andrew Gelman and Donald B. Rubin. Inference from iterative simulation using multiple sequences. *Statistical Science*, 7(4):457–511, 1992. DOI: 10.1214/ss/1177011136 35

Peter E. Hart, Nils J. Nilsson, and Bertram Raphael. A formal basis for the heuristic determination of minimum cost paths. *IEEE Trans. Systems Science and Cybernetics*, 4(2):100–107, 1968. DOI: 10.1109/TSSC.1968.300136 27

W. K. Hastings. Monte Carlo sampling methods using Markov chains and their applications. *Biometrika*, 57(1):97–109, 1970. DOI: 10.1093/biomet/57.1.97 34, 35

Ming Hua, Jian Pei, Wenjie Zhang, and Xuemin Lin. Ranking queries on uncertain data: a probabilistic threshold approach. In *Proc. ACM SIGMOD Int. Conf. on Management of Data*, pages 673–686, 2008. DOI: 10.1145/1376616.1376685 6, 21, 39, 40, 54

Ihab F. Ilyas, Walid G. Aref, and Ahmed K. Elmagarmid. Supporting top-k join queries in relational databases. *VLDB J.*, 13(3):207–221, 2004a. DOI: 10.1007/s00778-004-0128-2 47

Ihab F. Ilyas, Rahul Shah, Walid G. Aref, Jeffrey Scott Vitter, and Ahmed K. Elmagarmid. Rank-aware query optimization. In *Proc. ACM SIGMOD Int. Conf. on Management of Data*, pages 203–214, 2004b. DOI: 10.1145/1007568.1007593 49, 61

Tomasz Imieliński and Jr. Witold Lipski. Incomplete information in relational databases. *J. ACM*, 31(4):761–791, 1984. DOI: 10.1145/1634.1886 9

Claire Kenyon-Mathieu and Warren Schudy. How to rank with few errors. In *Proc. 39th Annual ACM Symp. on Theory of Computing*, pages 95–103, 2007. DOI: 10.1145/1250790.1250806 44

Jian Li and Amol Deshpande. Consensus answers for queries over probabilistic databases. In *Proc. 28th ACM SIGACT-SIGMOD-SIGART Symp. on Principles of Database Systems*, pages 259–268, 2009. DOI: 10.1145/1559795.1559835 6, 14, 15, 23, 24, 37, 43, 45, 46

Jian Li and Amol Deshpande. Ranking continuous probabilistic datasets. In *Proc. 36th Int. Conf. on Very Large Data Bases*, pages 638–649, 2010. 6

Jian Li, Barna Saha, and Amol Deshpande. A unified approach to ranking in probabilistic databases. pages 502–513, 2009. 6, 37, 38

Rajeev Motwani and Prabhakar Raghavan. *Randomized Algorithms*. Cambridge University Press, 1997. 18

Apostol Natsev, Yuan-Chi Chang, John R. Smith, Chung-Sheng Li, and Jeffrey Scott Vitter. Supporting incremental join queries on ranked inputs. In *Proc. 27th Int. Conf. on Very Large Data Bases*, pages 281–290, 2001. 47, 49

Dianne P. O'Leary. Multidimensional integration: Partition and conquer. *Computing in Science and Engineering*, 6(6):58–66, 2004. DOI: 10.1109/MCSE.2004.71 18

Christopher Ré, Nilesh N. Dalvi, and Dan Suciu. Efficient top-k query evaluation on probabilistic data. In *Proc. 23rd Int. Conf. on Data Engineering*, pages 886–895, 2007. DOI: 10.1109/ICDE.2007.367934 39

Matthew Richardson and Pedro Domingos. Markov logic networks. *Machine Learning*, 62(1-2): 107–136, 2006. DOI: 10.1007/s10994-006-5833-1 12

Anish Das Sarma, Omar Benjelloun, Alon Halevy, and Jennifer Widom. Working models for uncertain data. In *Proc. 22nd Int. Conf. on Data Engineering*, page 7, 2006. DOI: 10.1109/ICDE.2006.174 1, 9

Karl Schnaitter and Neoklis Polyzotis. Evaluating rank joins with optimal cost. In *Proc. 27th ACM SIGACT-SIGMOD-SIGART Symp. on Principles of Database Systems*, pages 43–52, 2008. DOI: 10.1145/1376916.1376924 49

Prithviraj Sen and Amol Deshpande. Representing and querying correlated tuples in probabilistic databases. In *Proc. 23rd Int. Conf. on Data Engineering*, pages 596–605, 2007. DOI: 10.1109/ICDE.2007.367905 10, 11

Mohamed A. Soliman and Ihab F. Ilyas. Ranking with uncertain scores. In *Proc. 25th Int. Conf. on Data Engineering*, pages 317–328, 2009. DOI: 10.1109/ICDE.2009.102 6, 16, 17, 20, 21, 23, 24, 30, 31, 33, 39, 43, 44

Mohamed A. Soliman, Ihab F. Ilyas, and Shalev Ben-David. Supporting ranking queries on uncertain and incomplete data. *VLDB J.*, 19(4), 2010a. DOI: 10.1007/s00778-009-0176-8 6, 16, 23, 24, 27, 30, 31, 33, 43, 44, 45

Mohamed A. Soliman, Ihab F. Ilyas, and Kevin C. Chang. Top-k query processing in uncertain databases. In *Proc. 23rd Int. Conf. on Data Engineering*, pages 896–905, 2007. 6, 7, 9, 20, 21, 27, 28, 29, 36, 39

Mohamed A. Soliman, Ihab F. Ilyas, and Kevin C. Chang. Probabilistic top-k and ranking-aggregate queries. *ACM Trans. Database Syst.*, 33(3):1–54, 2008. DOI: 10.1145/1386118.1386119 6, 9, 27, 28, 29

Mohamed A. Soliman, Ihab F. Ilyas, and Mina Saleeb. Building ranked mashups of unstructured sources with uncertain information. In *Proc. 36th Int. Conf. on Very Large Data Bases*, pages 826–837, 2010b. 6, 47, 50, 51, 54, 56

Yufei Tao, Xiaokui Xiao, and Jian Pei. Efficient skyline and top-k retrieval in subspaces. *IEEE Trans. Knowl. and Data Eng.*, 19(8):1072–1088, 2007. DOI: 10.1109/TKDE.2007.1051 5

P. van Acker. Transitivity revisited. *Ann. Oper. Res.*, 23(1-4):1–35, 1990. DOI: 10.1007/BF02204837 45

Michael L. Wick, Andrew McCallum, and Gerome Miklau. Scalable probabilistic databases with factor graphs and mcmc. In *Proc. 36th Int. Conf. on Very Large Data Bases*, pages 794–804, 2010. 12

Garrett Wolf, Hemal Khatri, Bhaumik Chokshi, Jianchun Fan, Yi Chen, and Subbarao Kambham-pati. Query processing over incomplete autonomous databases. In *Proc. 33rd Int. Conf. on Very Large Data Bases*, pages 1167–1190, 2007. DOI: 10.1109/ICDE.2007.369028 5

Xi Zhang and Jan Chomicki. Semantics and evaluation of top- queries in probabilistic databases. *Distributed and Parallel Databases*, 26(1):67–126, 2009. DOI: 10.1007/s10619-009-7050-y 6, 21, 39, 54, 55

Microsoft Popfly: http://www.popfly.com/

Yahoo! Pipes: http://pipes.yahoo.com/

Google Mashup Editor: http://code.google.com/gme/

Simmen, David E., Reiss, Frederick, Li, Yunyao, Thalamati, Suresh. Enabling enterprise mashups over unstructured text feeds with InfoSphere MashupHub and SystemT. *SIGMOD*, 1123–1126, 2009. 56

Simmen, David E., Altinel, Mehmet, Markl, Volker, Padmanabhan, Sriram, and Singh, Ashutosh. Damia: data mashups for intranet applications. *SIGMOD*, 1171–1182, 2008.

Kushmerick, Nicholas, Weld, Daniel S., and Doorenbos, Robert B. Wrapper introduction for information extraction, *IJCAI97*, 1997. 57, 59, 60

Crescenzi, Valter, Mecca, Giansalvatore, and Merialdo, Paolo. RoadRunner: Towards authomatic data extraction from large web sites, *VLDB01*, 109–118, 2001. 59

Authors' Biographies

IHAB F. ILYAS

Ihab F. Ilyas is an Associate Professor of Computer Science at the University of Waterloo. He received his PhD in computer science from Purdue University, West Lafayette, in 2004. He holds BS and MS degrees in computer science from Alexandria University, Egypt. His main research is in the area of database systems, with special interest in top-k and rank-aware query processing, managing uncertain and probabilistic databases, self-managing databases, indexing techniques, and spatial databases. For more information and a list of publications, please visit Ihab's home page at http://www.cs.uwaterloo.ca/~ilyas.

MOHAMED A. SOLIMAN

Mohamed A. Soliman is a software engineer at Greenplum, where he works on building massively distributed database systems for efficient support of data warehousing and analytics. He received his PhD in computer science from University of Waterloo in 2010. He holds BS and MS degrees in computer science from Alexandria University, Egypt. His main research is in the area of rank-aware retrieval in relational databases, focusing primarily on supporting ranking queries on uncertain and probabilistic data. For more information and a list of publications, please visit Mohamed's home page at http://www.cs.uwaterloo.ca/~m2ali.

Printed in the United States
by Baker & Taylor Publisher Services